THE Pet Sitting
Professional's Organizer and Logbook

Nola Lee Kelsey

Soggy Nomad Press

Las Vegas, NV, USA

ISBN: 978-1-957532-34-9

Cover design by Nola Lee Kelsey

PROPERTY OF:

RETURN TO:

NAME:

PHONE:

EMAIL:

Pets are humanizing.

They remind us we have an obligation and responsibility to preserve and nurture and care for all life.

- James Cromwell

About Care Sheets 🐾

Caring for a family's pets and home is a tremendous responsibility for a sitter. Trusting you with their care is a tremendous leap of faith on behalf of a client. Get it right!

Some pet sitters will use the included care sheets to collect every detail, others will just use them as a quick checklist. See the following sample pages. It's all good. Make your Pet Sitting Organizer your own. Also, if you prioritize something more, use the notes sections. The more you 'sit' the more refined you initial Client Meetups (a.k.a. Meet and Greets) will become and the more professional you will be.

Asking detailed questions is the first step towards being a pro, getting it right for your clients and their beloved pets. Showing people professionalism upfront instills in them a sence of peace of mind. Not to mention that during your stay having to riffle through someone's private spaces to find a roll of paper towels or a mop bucket is just awkward.

Tips

Repeat it! Ask clients to leave a printout of their travel itinerary, the daily routine for pets and other information they feel you may need. Why? Initial Meetups may happen days or weeks before your actual 'sit.' You may do multiple Meetups in a week, all while pet sitting. At times gig details can blur together. Write it down. Have your client write it down.

Additionally, a client's life can get hectic as a trip approaches. A gentle 'cajoling' to get them thinking about their pets and your needs just before leaving refocuses priorities. My first sit was with a 120 lb. Great Dane with separation anxiety, so I could not leave. I arrived to discover only 4 sheets of toilet paper in the entire house. Lesson learned.

Manage expectations! If you will be gone during the day discuss your client's expectations upfront. In fact, disuse them before you make an appointment for the initial Meetup. Don't waste their time or yours. If an owner wants you with their fur kids 22 hours a day and you work outside the house, take a pass on the assignment. Leave it for a sitter who can accommodate the client's needs. Keeping, and growing, people's trust in hiring house/pet sitters is good for all of us in the caregiver industry.

Clean it up! Leave the client's home slightly cleaner than you found it. People may not realize they've left things messy in the craziness of leaving on a trip. I've been know to take photos to document major messes when I arrive, in case they need reminding later. If I am asked to leave before they return, I may also take photos to document the condition I left their home in.

Personally, I am a dreadful housekeeper and I won't let a client use me as a maid. However, I do go a bit above and beyond just maintaining their home. Adding some extra touches pays off. Perhaps scrub a years worth of nose prints off the sliding glass doors or wash the dog beds. Clients may not always recognize exactly what you have done, but they can sence that the place looks a little bit nicer upon their return. You'll be rewarded in reviews.

Client

SAMPLE

NAME: Nola Kelsey

KEY/CODE: Under mat

ADDRESS: 7277 Anderson RD. Black Hawk

PHONE: 775-555-21212

STAY DATES/TIMES: Feb 5. 8am - Feb 12 5:30pm

STAY DATES/TIMES:

STAY DATES/TIMES:

NOTES:

🐾 Pet Care

PET: Rocko   DESC: Black Portie Mix. 3 years. neutered

PET: Betty Sue   DESC: Black and White PWD. 8 mo. spayed

PET: Ginger   DESC: Orange tabby cat 7 years. spayed

PET: DESC:

PET: DESC:

FEEDING

PET(S): Rocko   TIME(S): 7am & 5pm   AMOUNT: 1 scoop   FOOD: Urinary Form.

PET(S): Betty   TIME(S): 7am & 5pm   AMOUNT: 1.25 scps   FOOD: Puppy Form.

PET(S): Ginger   TIME(S): Auto Feeder   AMOUNT: FOOD:

MEDICATION

PET: Betty   MED: Doxi   DOSE: 1/2 pill. 2x daily after meals. use pill pocket

PET: MED: DOSE:

PET: MED: DOSE:

PET: MED: DOSE:

WALKS: 1x daily after morning meal.   💩 DISPOSAL: Scoop & bucket out back door

VETERINARIAN: Dr. Browne at Noah's Ark Vet Clinic

ADDRESS: 12 Deadwood Ave. Ste #4a. Rapid City   PHONE: 605-555-2121

ISSUES: Be sure not to pet or reinforce Betty Sue when she jumps on you.

CARE NOTES: **Trainer comes Tuesday mornings at 10 for 1- hour.

HOME CARE 🏠

Where, When &/or How To

EMERGENCY CONTACT: Kellie Walker (In-Law) 605-555-2222

ROOM: Guest Rm   WIFI: GBH-3A   PASSWORD: Way2Easy   TV/Remote: Lounge Pocket

TRASH: Pantry   CLEANING SUPPLIES: Hall Closet   VACUUM/MOP: Garage

WATER: Kitchen Filtered   COFFEE MAKER: Uses Pods   FURNACE, A/C: Nest in Master Ba

LAUNDRY: Leave washer door open when not in use   DISHWASHER: Out of order

UTILITY SHUTOFFS: H2O/ by gate. Fuse box in garage   MAIL: Box #2. Leave on desk

PLANT CARE: Yard on auto sprinklers. Kitchen has 3 succulents. Water light 1x per wk.

OTHER: Take large trash cans to curb on Tues night

AFTER NOTES: Trainier did no show, no call. but great sit overall. Would do again! Planet Gym 4 blocks away on Columbia St.

★★★★☆

Client

MEET-UP: 3/5 @ 2:30

NAME: Lisa & Jeb Webber

KEY/CODE: #3423

ADDRESS: 512 S. Joes Dr

PHONE: 777-555-1212

STAY DATES/TIMES: 3/17/23 4pm to 4/8/23 7pm

STAY DATES/TIMES:

STAY DATES/TIMES:

NOTES:

🐾 Pet Care

PET: Pebbles	DESC: Female Great Dane, 13 months, not fixed			
PET: Bam Bam	DESC: Male Dane, 3 years old, neutered			
PET:	DESC:			
PET:	DESC:			
PET:	DESC:			

FEEDING	PET(S): Pebbles & Bam	TIME(S): 8am, 5pm	AMOUNT: 2 cups	FOOD: Kibble w wet
	PET(S):	TIME(S):	AMOUNT:	FOOD:
	PET(S):	TIME(S):	AMOUNT:	FOOD:

MEDICATION	PET:	MED:	DOSE:
	PET:	MED:	DOSE:
	PET:	MED:	DOSE:
	PET:	MED:	DOSE:

WALKS: 💩 DISPOSAL:

VETERINARIAN: Lisa Webber is Vet - all Webber Vet Hosptical

ADDRESS: 21 Carson Way, Las Vegas, NV   PHONE: 777-555-4444

ISSUES: Crate at night to keep from chewing furniture.

CARE NOTES: Dry food is in white tubs in crates. ans on ounter. Mix 2 cups dog dry w 1/2 can per meal. Add 1 scoop Probioti Gravy Powder in A.M.

HOME CARE 🏠

EMERGENCY CONTACT: Tracy @ Webber Vet Hospital   777-555-4444

Where, When &/or How To			
ROOM: Master	WIFI: C-Tempest PASSWORD: azzie55!		TV/Remote:
TRASH: ✓	CLEANING SUPPLIES: pantry		VACUUM/MOP: On hall charger
WATER:	COFFEE MAKER: ✓		FURNACE, A/C: ✓
LAUNDRY: ✓			DISHWASHER:
UTILITY SHUTOFFS: ✓			MAIL:
PLANT CARE:			

OTHER: ✓ = Showed me. No mop, use Swify. Do not collect mail, held at PO

AFTER NOTES: Bam Bam went into heat during sit! Cratted her often but spent a lot of time scrubbing floors. Client had 3 cats not declared on App. Said autofed, but food ran out & still had to care for them NEVER AGAIN ★★☆☆☆

December 2023

SAMPLE

Sunday	Monday	Tuesday	Wednesday	Thursday	Friday	Saturday
26	27	28 Harley 7am.	29	30	1	2 End Harley 11 am.
		← Harley/Kim Watson 129 S. 8th St →				
3 Meetup Dan Smith (Bruno) 2 pm, 27 Baxter Ave	4	5	6	7 Bam Bam & Pebbles 6:30 am.	8	9
				← Bam Bam & Pebbles ────────		
10	11	12 Meetup Anita K. (Bear & Sassy) 11am 1022 E Avarado		14	15	16 End Bam Bam & Pebbles 5 pm.
	← /Kim Taylor, 2596 Jefferson St. Gate: #1212 ──────────────→					
17 Bruno 6 pm	18	19	20	21 End Bruno 10:30 am	22	23
	← Bruno/Dan S. 27 Baxter Ave →					
24	25 Pebbles & Bam Bam /Kim Taylor, 2596 Jefferson	26	27	28 Meetup Lisa Henderson (Zippy, Nino & Sam) 4:30 pm, 19028 Erikson Ranch Rd	29	30
	← Gate: #1212 ────→					
31	1	2	3	4	5	6

NOTES: Have ID for Gaurd Gate and get parking tag for Henderson Meetup on the 28th

Care Sheets

Client

NAME: _____ KEY/CODE: _____

ADDRESS: _____ PHONE: _____

STAY DATES/TIMES: _____

STAY DATES/TIMES: _____

STAY DATES/TIMES: _____

NOTES: _____

☙ Pet Care

PET:	DESC:		
PET:	DESC:		
PET:	DESC:		
PET:	DESC:		
PET:	DESC:		

PET(S):	TIME(S):	AMOUNT:	FOOD:
PET(S):	TIME(S):	AMOUNT:	FOOD:
PET(S):	TIME(S):	AMOUNT:	FOOD:

FEEDING

PET:	MED:	DOSE:
PET:	MED:	DOSE:
PET:	MED:	DOSE:
PET:	MED:	DOSE:

MEDICATION

WALKS: _____ 💩 DISPOSAL: _____

VETERINARIAN: _____

ADDRESS: _____ PHONE: _____

ISSUES: _____

CARE NOTES: _____

HOME CARE ⌂

EMERGENCY CONTACT: _____

Where, When &/or How To

ROOM:	WIFI:	PASSWORD:	TV/Remote:
TRASH:	CLEANING SUPPLIES:		VACUUM/MOP:
WATER:	COFFEE MAKER:		FURNACE, A/C:
LAUNDRY:			DISHWASHER:
UTILITY SHUTOFFS:			MAIL:

PLANT CARE: _____

OTHER: _____

AFTER NOTES: _____

☆ ☆ ☆ ☆ ☆

Client

MEET-UP: _____

NAME: _____
KEY/CODE: _____

ADDRESS: _____
PHONE: _____

STAY DATES/TIMES: _____

STAY DATES/TIMES: _____

STAY DATES/TIMES: _____

NOTES: _____

🐾 Pet Care

PET:	DESC:		
PET:	DESC:		
PET:	DESC:		
PET:	DESC:		
PET:	DESC:		

FEEDING

PET(S):	TIME(S):	AMOUNT:	FOOD:
PET(S):	TIME(S):	AMOUNT:	FOOD:
PET(S):	TIME(S):	AMOUNT:	FOOD:

MEDICATION

PET:	MED:	DOSE:
PET:	MED:	DOSE:
PET:	MED:	DOSE:
PET:	MED:	DOSE:

WALKS: _____   💩 DISPOSAL: _____

VETERINARIAN: _____

ADDRESS: _____   PHONE: _____

ISSUES: _____

CARE NOTES: _____

HOME CARE 🏠

EMERGENCY CONTACT: _____

Where, When &/or How To

ROOM:	WIFI:	PASSWORD:	TV/Remote:
TRASH:	CLEANING SUPPLIES:		VACUUM/MOP:
WATER:	COFFEE MAKER:		FURNACE, A/C:
LAUNDRY:			DISHWASHER:
UTILITY SHUTOFFS:			MAIL:

PLANT CARE: _____

OTHER: _____

AFTER NOTES: _____

☆ ☆ ☆ ☆ ☆

MEET-UP:＿＿＿＿＿＿＿＿＿＿

Client

NAME: ＿＿＿＿＿＿＿＿＿＿＿＿＿＿＿＿＿＿＿＿ KEY/CODE: ＿＿＿＿＿＿＿

ADDRESS: ＿＿＿＿＿＿＿＿＿＿＿＿＿＿＿＿＿＿＿ PHONE: ＿＿＿＿＿＿＿＿＿

STAY DATES/TIMES: ＿＿＿＿＿＿＿＿＿＿＿＿＿＿＿＿＿＿＿＿＿＿＿＿＿＿

STAY DATES/TIMES: ＿＿＿＿＿＿＿＿＿＿＿＿＿＿＿＿＿＿＿＿＿＿＿＿＿＿

STAY DATES/TIMES: ＿＿＿＿＿＿＿＿＿＿＿＿＿＿＿＿＿＿＿＿＿＿＿＿＿＿

NOTES: ＿＿＿＿＿＿＿＿＿＿＿＿＿＿＿＿＿＿＿＿＿＿＿＿＿＿＿＿＿＿＿＿

🐾 Pet Care

PET: ＿＿＿＿＿＿＿＿＿＿ DESC: ＿＿＿＿＿＿＿＿＿＿＿＿＿＿＿＿＿＿

PET: ＿＿＿＿＿＿＿＿＿＿ DESC: ＿＿＿＿＿＿＿＿＿＿＿＿＿＿＿＿＿＿

PET: ＿＿＿＿＿＿＿＿＿＿ DESC: ＿＿＿＿＿＿＿＿＿＿＿＿＿＿＿＿＿＿

PET: ＿＿＿＿＿＿＿＿＿＿ DESC: ＿＿＿＿＿＿＿＿＿＿＿＿＿＿＿＿＿＿

PET: ＿＿＿＿＿＿＿＿＿＿ DESC: ＿＿＿＿＿＿＿＿＿＿＿＿＿＿＿＿＿＿

FEEDING

PET(S): ＿＿＿＿＿＿ TIME(S): ＿＿＿＿ AMOUNT: ＿＿＿ FOOD: ＿＿＿

PET(S): ＿＿＿＿＿＿ TIME(S): ＿＿＿＿ AMOUNT: ＿＿＿ FOOD: ＿＿＿

PET(S): ＿＿＿＿＿＿ TIME(S): ＿＿＿＿ AMOUNT: ＿＿＿ FOOD: ＿＿＿

MEDICATION

PET: ＿＿＿ MED: ＿＿＿ DOSE: ＿＿＿＿＿＿＿＿＿＿＿

PET: ＿＿＿ MED: ＿＿＿ DOSE: ＿＿＿＿＿＿＿＿＿＿＿

PET: ＿＿＿ MED: ＿＿＿ DOSE: ＿＿＿＿＿＿＿＿＿＿＿

PET: ＿＿＿ MED: ＿＿＿ DOSE: ＿＿＿＿＿＿＿＿＿＿＿

WALKS: ＿＿＿＿＿＿＿＿＿ 💩 DISPOSAL: ＿＿＿＿＿

VETERINARIAN: ＿＿＿＿＿＿＿＿＿＿＿＿＿＿＿＿＿＿＿

ADDRESS: ＿＿＿＿＿＿＿＿＿＿＿ PHONE: ＿＿＿＿＿＿

ISSUES: ＿＿＿＿＿＿＿＿＿＿＿＿＿＿＿＿＿＿＿＿＿＿＿＿

CARE NOTES: ＿＿＿＿＿＿＿＿＿＿＿＿＿＿＿＿＿＿＿＿＿

HOME CARE 🏠

Where, When &/or How To

EMERGENCY CONTACT: ＿＿＿＿＿＿＿＿＿＿＿＿＿＿

ROOM: ＿＿＿ WIFI: ＿＿＿ PASSWORD: ＿＿＿ TV/Remote: ＿＿

TRASH: ＿＿ CLEANING SUPPLIES: ＿＿ VACUUM/MOP: ＿＿

WATER: ＿＿ COFFEE MAKER: ＿＿ FURNACE, A/C: ＿＿

LAUNDRY: ＿＿＿＿＿＿＿＿ DISHWASHER: ＿＿

UTILITY SHUTOFFS: ＿＿＿＿＿ MAIL: ＿＿

PLANT CARE: ＿＿＿＿＿＿＿＿＿＿＿＿＿＿

OTHER: ＿＿＿＿＿＿＿＿＿＿＿＿＿＿＿＿＿＿

AFTER NOTES: ＿＿＿＿＿＿＿＿＿＿＿＿＿＿＿＿＿＿

☆ ☆ ☆ ☆ ☆

Client

MEET-UP: _____

NAME: _____   KEY/CODE: _____

ADDRESS: _____   PHONE: _____

STAY DATES/TIMES: _____

STAY DATES/TIMES: _____

STAY DATES/TIMES: _____

NOTES: _____

🐾 Pet Care

PET:	DESC:		
PET:	DESC:		
PET:	DESC:		
PET:	DESC:		
PET:	DESC:		

FEEDING

PET(S):	TIME(S):	AMOUNT:	FOOD:
PET(S):	TIME(S):	AMOUNT:	FOOD:
PET(S):	TIME(S):	AMOUNT:	FOOD:

MEDICATION

PET:	MED:	DOSE:
PET:	MED:	DOSE:
PET:	MED:	DOSE:
PET:	MED:	DOSE:

WALKS: _____ 💩 DISPOSAL: _____

VETERINARIAN: _____

ADDRESS: _____ PHONE: _____

ISSUES: _____

CARE NOTES: _____

HOME CARE 🏠

Where, When &/or How To

EMERGENCY CONTACT: _____

ROOM: _____ WIFI: _____ PASSWORD: _____ TV/Remote: _____

TRASH: _____ CLEANING SUPPLIES: _____ VACUUM/MOP: _____

WATER: _____ COFFEE MAKER: _____ FURNACE, A/C: _____

LAUNDRY: _____ DISHWASHER: _____

UTILITY SHUTOFFS: _____ MAIL: _____

PLANT CARE: _____

OTHER: _____

AFTER NOTES: _____

☆ ☆ ☆ ☆ ☆

MEET-UP: _____

Client

NAME: _____   KEY/CODE: _____

ADDRESS: _____   PHONE: _____

STAY DATES/TIMES: _____

STAY DATES/TIMES: _____

STAY DATES/TIMES: _____

NOTES: _____

🐾 Pet Care

PET: _____   DESC: _____

PET: _____   DESC: _____

PET: _____   DESC: _____

PET: _____   DESC: _____

PET: _____   DESC: _____

FEEDING

PET(S): _____   TIME(S): _____   AMOUNT: _____   FOOD: _____

PET(S): _____   TIME(S): _____   AMOUNT: _____   FOOD: _____

PET(S): _____   TIME(S): _____   AMOUNT: _____   FOOD: _____

MEDICATION

PET: _____   MED: _____   DOSE: _____

PET: _____   MED: _____   DOSE: _____

PET: _____   MED: _____   DOSE: _____

PET: _____   MED: _____   DOSE: _____

WALKS: _____   💩 DISPOSAL: _____

VETERINARIAN: _____

ADDRESS: _____   PHONE: _____

ISSUES: _____

CARE NOTES: _____

HOME CARE 🏠

EMERGENCY CONTACT: _____

Where, When &/or How To

ROOM: _____   WIFI: _____   PASSWORD: _____   TV/Remote: _____

TRASH: _____   CLEANING SUPPLIES: _____   VACUUM/MOP: _____

WATER: _____   COFFEE MAKER: _____   FURNACE, A/C: _____

LAUNDRY: _____   DISHWASHER: _____

UTILITY SHUTOFFS: _____   MAIL: _____

PLANT CARE: _____

OTHER: _____

AFTER NOTES: _____

☆ ☆ ☆ ☆ ☆

Client

MEET-UP: _____

NAME: _____

KEY/CODE: _____

ADDRESS: _____

PHONE: _____

STAY DATES/TIMES: _____

STAY DATES/TIMES: _____

STAY DATES/TIMES: _____

NOTES: _____

🐾 Pet Care

PET: _____ DESC: _____

PET: _____ DESC: _____

PET: _____ DESC: _____

PET: _____ DESC: _____

PET: _____ DESC: _____

FEEDING

PET(S): _____ TIME(S): _____ AMOUNT: _____ FOOD: _____

PET(S): _____ TIME(S): _____ AMOUNT: _____ FOOD: _____

PET(S): _____ TIME(S): _____ AMOUNT: _____ FOOD: _____

MEDICATION

PET: _____ MED: _____ DOSE: _____

PET: _____ MED: _____ DOSE: _____

PET: _____ MED: _____ DOSE: _____

PET: _____ MED: _____ DOSE: _____

WALKS: _____ 💩 DISPOSAL: _____

VETERINARIAN: _____

ADDRESS: _____ PHONE: _____

ISSUES: _____

CARE NOTES: _____

HOME CARE 🏠

Where, When &/or How To

EMERGENCY CONTACT: _____

ROOM: _____ WIFI: _____ PASSWORD: _____ TV/Remote: _____

TRASH: _____ CLEANING SUPPLIES: _____ VACUUM/MOP: _____

WATER: _____ COFFEE MAKER: _____ FURNACE, A/C: _____

LAUNDRY: _____ DISHWASHER: _____

UTILITY SHUTOFFS: _____ MAIL: _____

PLANT CARE: _____

OTHER: _____

AFTER NOTES: _____

☆ ☆ ☆ ☆ ☆

Client

NAME: KEY/CODE:

ADDRESS: PHONE:

STAY DATES/TIMES:

STAY DATES/TIMES:

STAY DATES/TIMES:

NOTES:

❀ Pet Care

PET: DESC:

PET: DESC:

PET: DESC:

PET: DESC:

PET: DESC:

FEEDING

PET(S):   TIME(S):   AMOUNT: FOOD:

PET(S):   TIME(S):   AMOUNT: FOOD:

PET(S):   TIME(S):   AMOUNT: FOOD:

MEDICATION

PET: MED: DOSE:

PET: MED: DOSE:

PET: MED: DOSE:

PET: MED: DOSE:

WALKS: 💩 DISPOSAL:

VETERINARIAN:

ADDRESS: PHONE:

ISSUES:

CARE NOTES:

HOME CARE 🏠

Where, When &/or How To

EMERGENCY CONTACT:

ROOM: WIFI: PASSWORD: TV/Remote:

TRASH: CLEANING SUPPLIES: VACUUM/MOP:

WATER: COFFEE MAKER: FURNACE, A/C:

LAUNDRY: DISHWASHER:

UTILITY SHUTOFFS: MAIL:

PLANT CARE:

OTHER:

AFTER NOTES:

☆ ☆ ☆ ☆ ☆

Client

MEET-UP: _____

NAME: _____ KEY/CODE: _____

ADDRESS: _____ PHONE: _____

STAY DATES/TIMES: _____

STAY DATES/TIMES: _____

STAY DATES/TIMES: _____

NOTES: _____

🐾 Pet Care

PET:	DESC:		
PET:	DESC:		
PET:	DESC:		
PET:	DESC:		
PET:	DESC:		

FEEDING

PET(S):	TIME(S):	AMOUNT:	FOOD:
PET(S):	TIME(S):	AMOUNT:	FOOD:
PET(S):	TIME(S):	AMOUNT:	FOOD:

MEDICATION

PET:	MED:	DOSE:
PET:	MED:	DOSE:
PET:	MED:	DOSE:
PET:	MED:	DOSE:

WALKS: _____ 💩 DISPOSAL: _____

VETERINARIAN: _____

ADDRESS: _____ PHONE: _____

ISSUES: _____

CARE NOTES: _____

HOME CARE 🏠

Where, When &/or How To

EMERGENCY CONTACT: _____

ROOM: _____ WIFI: _____ PASSWORD: _____ TV/Remote: _____

TRASH: _____ CLEANING SUPPLIES: _____ VACUUM/MOP: _____

WATER: _____ COFFEE MAKER: _____ FURNACE, A/C: _____

LAUNDRY: _____ DISHWASHER: _____

UTILITY SHUTOFFS: _____ MAIL: _____

PLANT CARE: _____

OTHER: _____

AFTER NOTES: _____

☆ ☆ ☆ ☆ ☆

MEET-UP: _____

Client

NAME: _____ KEY/CODE: _____

ADDRESS: _____ PHONE: _____

STAY DATES/TIMES: _____

STAY DATES/TIMES: _____

STAY DATES/TIMES: _____

NOTES: _____

🐾 Pet Care

PET: _____ DESC: _____

PET: _____ DESC: _____

PET: _____ DESC: _____

PET: _____ DESC: _____

PET: _____ DESC: _____

PET(S):	TIME(S):	AMOUNT:	FOOD:
PET(S):	TIME(S):	AMOUNT:	FOOD:
PET(S):	TIME(S):	AMOUNT:	FOOD:

FEEDING

PET: _____ MED: _____ DOSE: _____

PET: _____ MED: _____ DOSE: _____

PET: _____ MED: _____ DOSE: _____

PET: _____ MED: _____ DOSE: _____

MEDICATION

WALKS: _____ 💩 DISPOSAL: _____

VETERINARIAN: _____

ADDRESS: _____ PHONE: _____

ISSUES: _____

CARE NOTES: _____

HOME CARE 🏠

EMERGENCY CONTACT: _____

ROOM: _____ WIFI: _____ PASSWORD: _____ TV/Remote: _____

TRASH: _____ CLEANING SUPPLIES: _____ VACUUM/MOP: _____

WATER: _____ COFFEE MAKER: _____ FURNACE, A/C: _____

LAUNDRY: _____ DISHWASHER: _____

UTILITY SHUTOFFS: _____ MAIL: _____

PLANT CARE: _____

OTHER: _____

Where, When &/or How To

AFTER NOTES: _____

☆ ☆ ☆ ☆ ☆

Client

MEET-UP: _____

NAME: _____   KEY/CODE: _____

ADDRESS: _____   PHONE: _____

STAY DATES/TIMES: _____

STAY DATES/TIMES: _____

STAY DATES/TIMES: _____

NOTES: _____

🐾 Pet Care

PET: _____   DESC: _____

PET: _____   DESC: _____

PET: _____   DESC: _____

PET: _____   DESC: _____

PET: _____   DESC: _____

FEEDING

PET(S): _____   TIME(S): _____   AMOUNT: _____   FOOD: _____

PET(S): _____   TIME(S): _____   AMOUNT: _____   FOOD: _____

PET(S): _____   TIME(S): _____   AMOUNT: _____   FOOD: _____

MEDICATION

PET: _____   MED: _____   DOSE: _____

PET: _____   MED: _____   DOSE: _____

PET: _____   MED: _____   DOSE: _____

PET: _____   MED: _____   DOSE: _____

WALKS: _____   💩 DISPOSAL: _____

VETERINARIAN: _____

ADDRESS: _____   PHONE: _____

ISSUES: _____

CARE NOTES: _____

HOME CARE 🏠

Where, When &/or How To

EMERGENCY CONTACT: _____

ROOM: _____   WIFI: _____   PASSWORD: _____   TV/Remote: _____

TRASH: _____   CLEANING SUPPLIES: _____   VACUUM/MOP: _____

WATER: _____   COFFEE MAKER: _____   FURNACE, A/C: _____

LAUNDRY: _____   DISHWASHER: _____

UTILITY SHUTOFFS: _____   MAIL: _____

PLANT CARE: _____

OTHER: _____

AFTER NOTES: _____

☆☆☆☆☆

MEET-UP: _____

Client

NAME: _____ KEY/CODE: _____

ADDRESS: _____ PHONE: _____

STAY DATES/TIMES: _____

STAY DATES/TIMES: _____

STAY DATES/TIMES: _____

NOTES: _____

🐾 Pet Care

PET: _____ DESC: _____

PET: _____ DESC: _____

PET: _____ DESC: _____

PET: _____ DESC: _____

PET: _____ DESC: _____

FEEDING

PET(S): _____ TIME(S): _____ AMOUNT: _____ FOOD: _____

PET(S): _____ TIME(S): _____ AMOUNT: _____ FOOD: _____

PET(S): _____ TIME(S): _____ AMOUNT: _____ FOOD: _____

MEDICATION

PET: _____ MED: _____ DOSE: _____

PET: _____ MED: _____ DOSE: _____

PET: _____ MED: _____ DOSE: _____

PET: _____ MED: _____ DOSE: _____

WALKS: _____ 💩 DISPOSAL: _____

VETERINARIAN: _____

ADDRESS: _____ PHONE: _____

ISSUES: _____

CARE NOTES: _____

HOME CARE 🏠

EMERGENCY CONTACT: _____

Where, When &/or How To

ROOM: _____ WIFI: _____ PASSWORD: _____ TV/Remote: _____

TRASH: _____ CLEANING SUPPLIES: _____ VACUUM/MOP: _____

WATER: _____ COFFEE MAKER: _____ FURNACE, A/C: _____

LAUNDRY: _____ DISHWASHER: _____

UTILITY SHUTOFFS: _____ MAIL: _____

PLANT CARE: _____

OTHER: _____

AFTER NOTES: _____

☆ ☆ ☆ ☆ ☆

Client

NAME: _____ KEY/CODE: _____

ADDRESS: _____ PHONE: _____

STAY DATES/TIMES: _____

STAY DATES/TIMES: _____

STAY DATES/TIMES: _____

NOTES: _____

🐾 Pet Care

PET:	DESC:		
PET:	DESC:		
PET:	DESC:		
PET:	DESC:		
PET:	DESC:		

FEEDING

PET(S):	TIME(S):	AMOUNT:	FOOD:
PET(S):	TIME(S):	AMOUNT:	FOOD:
PET(S):	TIME(S):	AMOUNT:	FOOD:

MEDICATION

PET:	MED:	DOSE:
PET:	MED:	DOSE:
PET:	MED:	DOSE:
PET:	MED:	DOSE:

WALKS: _____ 💩 DISPOSAL: _____

VETERINARIAN: _____

ADDRESS: _____ PHONE: _____

ISSUES: _____

CARE NOTES: _____

HOME CARE 🏠

Where, When &/or How To

EMERGENCY CONTACT: _____

ROOM: _____ WIFI: _____ PASSWORD: _____ TV/Remote: _____

TRASH: _____ CLEANING SUPPLIES: _____ VACUUM/MOP: _____

WATER: _____ COFFEE MAKER: _____ FURNACE, A/C: _____

LAUNDRY: _____ DISHWASHER: _____

UTILITY SHUTOFFS: _____ MAIL: _____

PLANT CARE: _____

OTHER: _____

AFTER NOTES: _____

☆ ☆ ☆ ☆ ☆

MEET-UP: _____   # Client

NAME: _____   KEY/CODE: _____

ADDRESS: _____   PHONE: _____

STAY DATES/TIMES: _____

STAY DATES/TIMES: _____

STAY DATES/TIMES: _____

NOTES: _____

❀ Pet Care

PET: _____ DESC: _____

PET: _____ DESC: _____

PET: _____ DESC: _____

PET: _____ DESC: _____

PET: _____ DESC: _____

	PET(S):	TIME(S):	AMOUNT:	FOOD:
FEEDING	PET(S):	TIME(S):	AMOUNT:	FOOD:
	PET(S):	TIME(S):	AMOUNT:	FOOD:

	PET:	MED:	DOSE:
MEDICATION	PET:	MED:	DOSE:
	PET:	MED:	DOSE:
	PET:	MED:	DOSE:

WALKS: _____ 💩 DISPOSAL: _____

VETERINARIAN: _____

ADDRESS: _____ PHONE: _____

ISSUES: _____

CARE NOTES: _____

HOME CARE 🏠

EMERGENCY CONTACT: _____

Where, When &/or How To	ROOM:	WIFI:	PASSWORD:	TV/Remote:
	TRASH:	CLEANING SUPPLIES:		VACUUM/MOP:
	WATER:	COFFEE MAKER:		FURNACE, A/C:
	LAUNDRY:			DISHWASHER:
	UTILITY SHUTOFFS:			MAIL:
	PLANT CARE:			

OTHER: _____

AFTER NOTES: _____

☆ ☆ ☆ ☆ ☆

Client

MEET-UP: _____

NAME: _____ KEY/CODE: _____

ADDRESS: _____ PHONE: _____

STAY DATES/TIMES: _____

STAY DATES/TIMES: _____

STAY DATES/TIMES: _____

NOTES: _____

🐾 Pet Care

PET: _____ DESC: _____

PET: _____ DESC: _____

PET: _____ DESC: _____

PET: _____ DESC: _____

PET: _____ DESC: _____

FEEDING

PET(S): _____ TIME(S): _____ AMOUNT: _____ FOOD: _____

PET(S): _____ TIME(S): _____ AMOUNT: _____ FOOD: _____

PET(S): _____ TIME(S): _____ AMOUNT: _____ FOOD: _____

MEDICATION

PET: _____ MED: _____ DOSE: _____

PET: _____ MED: _____ DOSE: _____

PET: _____ MED: _____ DOSE: _____

PET: _____ MED: _____ DOSE: _____

WALKS: _____ 💩 DISPOSAL: _____

VETERINARIAN: _____

ADDRESS: _____ PHONE: _____

ISSUES: _____

CARE NOTES: _____

HOME CARE 🏠

Where, When &/or How To

EMERGENCY CONTACT: _____

ROOM: _____ WIFI: _____ PASSWORD: _____ TV/Remote: _____

TRASH: _____ CLEANING SUPPLIES: _____ VACUUM/MOP: _____

WATER: _____ COFFEE MAKER: _____ FURNACE, A/C: _____

LAUNDRY: _____ DISHWASHER: _____

UTILITY SHUTOFFS: _____ MAIL: _____

PLANT CARE: _____

OTHER: _____

AFTER NOTES: _____

☆ ☆ ☆ ☆ ☆

Client

NAME: _____ KEY/CODE: _____

ADDRESS: _____ PHONE: _____

STAY DATES/TIMES: _____

STAY DATES/TIMES: _____

STAY DATES/TIMES: _____

NOTES: _____

❀ Pet Care

PET: _____ DESC: _____

PET: _____ DESC: _____

PET: _____ DESC: _____

PET: _____ DESC: _____

PET: _____ DESC: _____

FEEDING

PET(S): _____ TIME(S): _____ AMOUNT: _____ FOOD: _____

PET(S): _____ TIME(S): _____ AMOUNT: _____ FOOD: _____

PET(S): _____ TIME(S): _____ AMOUNT: _____ FOOD: _____

MEDICATION

PET: _____ MED: _____ DOSE: _____

PET: _____ MED: _____ DOSE: _____

PET: _____ MED: _____ DOSE: _____

PET: _____ MED: _____ DOSE: _____

WALKS: _____ 💩 DISPOSAL: _____

VETERINARIAN: _____

ADDRESS: _____ PHONE: _____

ISSUES: _____

CARE NOTES: _____

HOME CARE 🏠

EMERGENCY CONTACT: _____

Where, When &/or How To

ROOM: _____ WIFI: _____ PASSWORD: _____ TV/Remote: _____

TRASH: _____ CLEANING SUPPLIES: _____ VACUUM/MOP: _____

WATER: _____ COFFEE MAKER: _____ FURNACE, A/C: _____

LAUNDRY: _____ DISHWASHER: _____

UTILITY SHUTOFFS: _____ MAIL: _____

PLANT CARE: _____

OTHER: _____

AFTER NOTES: _____

☆ ☆ ☆ ☆ ☆

Client

NAME: _____ KEY/CODE: _____

ADDRESS: _____ PHONE: _____

STAY DATES/TIMES: _____

STAY DATES/TIMES: _____

STAY DATES/TIMES: _____

NOTES: _____

🐾 Pet Care

PET: _____ DESC: _____

PET: _____ DESC: _____

PET: _____ DESC: _____

PET: _____ DESC: _____

PET: _____ DESC: _____

	PET(S):	TIME(S):	AMOUNT:	FOOD:
FEEDING	PET(S):	TIME(S):	AMOUNT:	FOOD:
	PET(S):	TIME(S):	AMOUNT:	FOOD:

	PET:	MED:	DOSE:
	PET:	MED:	DOSE:
MEDICATION	PET:	MED:	DOSE:
	PET:	MED:	DOSE:

WALKS: _____ 💩 DISPOSAL: _____

VETERINARIAN: _____

ADDRESS: _____ PHONE: _____

ISSUES: _____

CARE NOTES: _____

HOME CARE 🏠

EMERGENCY CONTACT: _____

	ROOM:	WIFI:	PASSWORD:	TV/Remote:
	TRASH:	CLEANING SUPPLIES:	VACUUM/MOP:
Where, When &/or How To	WATER:	COFFEE MAKER:	FURNACE, A/C:
	LAUNDRY:		DISHWASHER:
	UTILITY SHUTOFFS:		MAIL:
	PLANT CARE:		

OTHER: _____

AFTER NOTES: _____

☆ ☆ ☆ ☆ ☆

MEET-UP: _____ **Client**

NAME: _____ KEY/CODE: _____

ADDRESS: _____ PHONE: _____

STAY DATES/TIMES: _____

STAY DATES/TIMES: _____

STAY DATES/TIMES: _____

NOTES: _____

☙ Pet Care

PET: _____ DESC: _____

PET: _____ DESC: _____

PET: _____ DESC: _____

PET: _____ DESC: _____

PET: _____ DESC: _____

FEEDING

PET(S): _____ TIME(S): _____ AMOUNT: _____ FOOD: _____

PET(S): _____ TIME(S): _____ AMOUNT: _____ FOOD: _____

PET(S): _____ TIME(S): _____ AMOUNT: _____ FOOD: _____

MEDICATION

PET: _____ MED: _____ DOSE: _____

PET: _____ MED: _____ DOSE: _____

PET: _____ MED: _____ DOSE: _____

PET: _____ MED: _____ DOSE: _____

WALKS: _____ 💩 DISPOSAL: _____

VETERINARIAN: _____

ADDRESS: _____ PHONE: _____

ISSUES: _____

CARE NOTES: _____

HOME CARE 🏠

Where, When &/or How To

EMERGENCY CONTACT: _____

ROOM: _____ WIFI: _____ PASSWORD: _____ TV/Remote: _____

TRASH: _____ CLEANING SUPPLIES: _____ VACUUM/MOP: _____

WATER: _____ COFFEE MAKER: _____ FURNACE, A/C: _____

LAUNDRY: _____ DISHWASHER: _____

UTILITY SHUTOFFS: _____ MAIL: _____

PLANT CARE: _____

OTHER: _____

AFTER NOTES: _____

☆ ☆ ☆ ☆ ☆

Client

MEET-UP: _____

NAME: _____
ADDRESS: _____
STAY DATES/TIMES: _____
STAY DATES/TIMES: _____
STAY DATES/TIMES: _____
NOTES: _____

KEY/CODE: _____
PHONE: _____

🐾 Pet Care

PET: _____ DESC: _____
PET: _____ DESC: _____
PET: _____ DESC: _____
PET: _____ DESC: _____
PET: _____ DESC: _____

FEEDING

PET(S): _____ TIME(S): _____ AMOUNT: _____ FOOD: _____
PET(S): _____ TIME(S): _____ AMOUNT: _____ FOOD: _____
PET(S): _____ TIME(S): _____ AMOUNT: _____ FOOD: _____

MEDICATION

PET: _____ MED: _____ DOSE: _____
PET: _____ MED: _____ DOSE: _____
PET: _____ MED: _____ DOSE: _____
PET: _____ MED: _____ DOSE: _____

WALKS: _____ 💩 DISPOSAL: _____
VETERINARIAN: _____
ADDRESS: _____ PHONE: _____
ISSUES: _____

CARE NOTES: _____

HOME CARE 🏠

Where, When &/or How To

EMERGENCY CONTACT: _____
ROOM: _____ WIFI: _____ PASSWORD: _____ TV/Remote: _____
TRASH: _____ CLEANING SUPPLIES: _____ VACUUM/MOP: _____
WATER: _____ COFFEE MAKER: _____ FURNACE, A/C: _____
LAUNDRY: _____ DISHWASHER: _____
UTILITY SHUTOFFS: _____ MAIL: _____
PLANT CARE: _____

OTHER: _____

AFTER NOTES: _____

☆ ☆ ☆ ☆ ☆

MEET-UP: _____

Client

NAME: _____ KEY/CODE: _____

ADDRESS: _____ PHONE: _____

STAY DATES/TIMES: _____

STAY DATES/TIMES: _____

STAY DATES/TIMES: _____

NOTES: _____

☙ Pet Care

PET:	DESC:			
PET:	DESC:			
PET:	DESC:			
PET:	DESC:			
PET:	DESC:			

	PET(S):	TIME(S):	AMOUNT:	FOOD:
FEEDING	PET(S):	TIME(S):	AMOUNT:	FOOD:
	PET(S):	TIME(S):	AMOUNT:	FOOD:

	PET:	MED:	DOSE:
MEDICATION	PET:	MED:	DOSE:
	PET:	MED:	DOSE:
	PET:	MED:	DOSE:

WALKS: _____ 💩 DISPOSAL: _____

VETERINARIAN: _____

ADDRESS: _____ PHONE: _____

ISSUES: _____

CARE NOTES: _____

HOME CARE 🏠

EMERGENCY CONTACT: _____

Where, When &/or How To	ROOM:	WIFI:	PASSWORD:	TV/Remote:
	TRASH:	CLEANING SUPPLIES:		VACUUM/MOP:
	WATER:	COFFEE MAKER:		FURNACE, A/C:
	LAUNDRY:			DISHWASHER:
	UTILITY SHUTOFFS:			MAIL:
	PLANT CARE:			

OTHER: _____

AFTER NOTES: _____

☆ ☆ ☆ ☆ ☆

Client

MEET-UP: _____

NAME: _____ KEY/CODE: _____

ADDRESS: _____ PHONE: _____

STAY DATES/TIMES: _____

STAY DATES/TIMES: _____

STAY DATES/TIMES: _____

NOTES: _____

🐾 Pet Care

PET: _____ DESC: _____

PET: _____ DESC: _____

PET: _____ DESC: _____

PET: _____ DESC: _____

PET: _____ DESC: _____

FEEDING

PET(S): _____ TIME(S): _____ AMOUNT: _____ FOOD: _____

PET(S): _____ TIME(S): _____ AMOUNT: _____ FOOD: _____

PET(S): _____ TIME(S): _____ AMOUNT: _____ FOOD: _____

MEDICATION

PET: _____ MED: _____ DOSE: _____

PET: _____ MED: _____ DOSE: _____

PET: _____ MED: _____ DOSE: _____

PET: _____ MED: _____ DOSE: _____

WALKS: _____ 💩 DISPOSAL: _____

VETERINARIAN: _____

ADDRESS: _____ PHONE: _____

ISSUES: _____

CARE NOTES: _____

HOME CARE 🏠

EMERGENCY CONTACT: _____

Where, When &/or How To

ROOM: _____ WIFI: _____ PASSWORD: _____ TV/Remote: _____

TRASH: _____ CLEANING SUPPLIES: _____ VACUUM/MOP: _____

WATER: _____ COFFEE MAKER: _____ FURNACE, A/C: _____

LAUNDRY: _____ DISHWASHER: _____

UTILITY SHUTOFFS: _____ MAIL: _____

PLANT CARE: _____

OTHER: _____

AFTER NOTES: _____

☆ ☆ ☆ ☆ ☆

MEET-UP: _____

Client

NAME: _____ KEY/CODE: _____

ADDRESS: _____ PHONE: _____

STAY DATES/TIMES: _____

STAY DATES/TIMES: _____

STAY DATES/TIMES: _____

NOTES: _____

🐾 Pet Care

PET: _____ DESC: _____

PET: _____ DESC: _____

PET: _____ DESC: _____

PET: _____ DESC: _____

PET: _____ DESC: _____

FEEDING

PET(S): _____ TIME(S): _____ AMOUNT: _____ FOOD: _____

PET(S): _____ TIME(S): _____ AMOUNT: _____ FOOD: _____

PET(S): _____ TIME(S): _____ AMOUNT: _____ FOOD: _____

MEDICATION

PET: _____ MED: _____ DOSE: _____

PET: _____ MED: _____ DOSE: _____

PET: _____ MED: _____ DOSE: _____

PET: _____ MED: _____ DOSE: _____

WALKS: _____ 💩 DISPOSAL: _____

VETERINARIAN: _____

ADDRESS: _____ PHONE: _____

ISSUES: _____

CARE NOTES: _____

HOME CARE 🏠

EMERGENCY CONTACT: _____

Where, When &/or How To

ROOM: _____ WIFI: _____ PASSWORD: _____ TV/Remote: _____

TRASH: _____ CLEANING SUPPLIES: _____ VACUUM/MOP: _____

WATER: _____ COFFEE MAKER: _____ FURNACE, A/C: _____

LAUNDRY: _____ DISHWASHER: _____

UTILITY SHUTOFFS: _____ MAIL: _____

PLANT CARE: _____

OTHER: _____

AFTER NOTES: _____

☆ ☆ ☆ ☆ ☆

Client

MEET–UP: _____

NAME: _____ KEY/CODE: _____

ADDRESS: _____ PHONE: _____

STAY DATES/TIMES: _____

STAY DATES/TIMES: _____

STAY DATES/TIMES: _____

NOTES: _____

🐾 Pet Care

PET: _____ DESC: _____

PET: _____ DESC: _____

PET: _____ DESC: _____

PET: _____ DESC: _____

PET: _____ DESC: _____

FEEDING

PET(S): _____ TIME(S): _____ AMOUNT: _____ FOOD: _____

PET(S): _____ TIME(S): _____ AMOUNT: _____ FOOD: _____

PET(S): _____ TIME(S): _____ AMOUNT: _____ FOOD: _____

MEDICATION

PET: _____ MED: _____ DOSE: _____

PET: _____ MED: _____ DOSE: _____

PET: _____ MED: _____ DOSE: _____

PET: _____ MED: _____ DOSE: _____

WALKS: _____ 💩 DISPOSAL: _____

VETERINARIAN: _____

ADDRESS: _____ PHONE: _____

ISSUES: _____

CARE NOTES: _____

HOME CARE 🏠

Where, When &/or How To

EMERGENCY CONTACT: _____

ROOM: _____ WIFI: _____ PASSWORD: _____ TV/Remote: _____

TRASH: _____ CLEANING SUPPLIES: _____ VACUUM/MOP: _____

WATER: _____ COFFEE MAKER: _____ FURNACE, A/C: _____

LAUNDRY: _____ DISHWASHER: _____

UTILITY SHUTOFFS: _____ MAIL: _____

PLANT CARE: _____

OTHER: _____

AFTER NOTES: _____

☆ ☆ ☆ ☆ ☆

Client

MEET-UP: _____

NAME: _____ KEY/CODE: _____

ADDRESS: _____ PHONE: _____

STAY DATES/TIMES: _____

STAY DATES/TIMES: _____

STAY DATES/TIMES: _____

NOTES: _____

🐾 Pet Care

FEEDING	PET: _____	DESC: _____

PET: _____ DESC: _____

PET: _____ DESC: _____

PET: _____ DESC: _____

PET: _____ DESC: _____

PET: _____ DESC: _____

PET(S): _____ TIME(S): _____ AMOUNT: _____ FOOD: _____

PET(S): _____ TIME(S): _____ AMOUNT: _____ FOOD: _____

PET(S): _____ TIME(S): _____ AMOUNT: _____ FOOD: _____

MEDICATION

PET: _____ MED: _____ DOSE: _____

PET: _____ MED: _____ DOSE: _____

PET: _____ MED: _____ DOSE: _____

PET: _____ MED: _____ DOSE: _____

WALKS: _____ 💩 DISPOSAL: _____

VETERINARIAN: _____

ADDRESS: _____ PHONE: _____

ISSUES: _____

CARE NOTES: _____

HOME CARE 🏠

Where, When &/or How To

EMERGENCY CONTACT: _____

ROOM: _____ WIFI: _____ PASSWORD: _____ TV/Remote: _____

TRASH: _____ CLEANING SUPPLIES: _____ VACUUM/MOP: _____

WATER: _____ COFFEE MAKER: _____ FURNACE, A/C: _____

LAUNDRY: _____ DISHWASHER: _____

UTILITY SHUTOFFS: _____ MAIL: _____

PLANT CARE: _____

OTHER: _____

AFTER NOTES: _____

☆ ☆ ☆ ☆ ☆

Client

MEET-UP: _____

NAME: _____ KEY/CODE: _____

ADDRESS: _____ PHONE: _____

STAY DATES/TIMES: _____

STAY DATES/TIMES: _____

STAY DATES/TIMES: _____

NOTES: _____

🐾 Pet Care

PET: _____ DESC: _____

PET: _____ DESC: _____

PET: _____ DESC: _____

PET: _____ DESC: _____

PET: _____ DESC: _____

FEEDING

PET(S): _____ TIME(S): _____ AMOUNT: _____ FOOD: _____

PET(S): _____ TIME(S): _____ AMOUNT: _____ FOOD: _____

PET(S): _____ TIME(S): _____ AMOUNT: _____ FOOD: _____

MEDICATION

PET: _____ MED: _____ DOSE: _____

PET: _____ MED: _____ DOSE: _____

PET: _____ MED: _____ DOSE: _____

PET: _____ MED: _____ DOSE: _____

WALKS: _____ 💩 DISPOSAL: _____

VETERINARIAN: _____

ADDRESS: _____ PHONE: _____

ISSUES: _____

CARE NOTES: _____

HOME CARE 🏠

Where, When &/or How To

EMERGENCY CONTACT: _____

ROOM: _____ WIFI: _____ PASSWORD: _____ TV/Remote: _____

TRASH: _____ CLEANING SUPPLIES: _____ VACUUM/MOP: _____

WATER: _____ COFFEE MAKER: _____ FURNACE, A/C: _____

LAUNDRY: _____ DISHWASHER: _____

UTILITY SHUTOFFS: _____ MAIL: _____

PLANT CARE: _____

OTHER: _____

AFTER NOTES: _____

☆ ☆ ☆ ☆ ☆

Client

NAME: _____   KEY/CODE: _____

ADDRESS: _____   PHONE: _____

STAY DATES/TIMES: _____

STAY DATES/TIMES: _____

STAY DATES/TIMES: _____

NOTES: _____

🐾 Pet Care

PET: _____   DESC: _____

PET: _____   DESC: _____

PET: _____   DESC: _____

PET: _____   DESC: _____

PET: _____   DESC: _____

FEEDING

PET(S): _____   TIME(S): _____   AMOUNT: _____   FOOD: _____

PET(S): _____   TIME(S): _____   AMOUNT: _____   FOOD: _____

PET(S): _____   TIME(S): _____   AMOUNT: _____   FOOD: _____

MEDICATION

PET: _____   MED: _____   DOSE: _____

PET: _____   MED: _____   DOSE: _____

PET: _____   MED: _____   DOSE: _____

PET: _____   MED: _____   DOSE: _____

WALKS: _____   💩 DISPOSAL: _____

VETERINARIAN: _____

ADDRESS: _____   PHONE: _____

ISSUES: _____

CARE NOTES: _____

HOME CARE 🏠

Where, When &/or How To

EMERGENCY CONTACT: _____

ROOM: _____   WIFI: _____   PASSWORD: _____   TV/Remote: _____

TRASH: _____   CLEANING SUPPLIES: _____   VACUUM/MOP: _____

WATER: _____   COFFEE MAKER: _____   FURNACE, A/C: _____

LAUNDRY: _____   DISHWASHER: _____

UTILITY SHUTOFFS: _____   MAIL: _____

PLANT CARE: _____

OTHER: _____

AFTER NOTES: _____

☆ ☆ ☆ ☆ ☆

Client

MEET-UP: _____

NAME: _____ KEY/CODE: _____

ADDRESS: _____ PHONE: _____

STAY DATES/TIMES: _____

STAY DATES/TIMES: _____

STAY DATES/TIMES: _____

NOTES: _____

🐾 Pet Care

PET:	DESC:		
PET:	DESC:		
PET:	DESC:		
PET:	DESC:		
PET:	DESC:		

FEEDING

PET(S):	TIME(S):	AMOUNT:	FOOD:
PET(S):	TIME(S):	AMOUNT:	FOOD:
PET(S):	TIME(S):	AMOUNT:	FOOD:

MEDICATION

PET:	MED:	DOSE:
PET:	MED:	DOSE:
PET:	MED:	DOSE:
PET:	MED:	DOSE:

WALKS: _____ 💩 DISPOSAL: _____

VETERINARIAN: _____

ADDRESS: _____ PHONE: _____

ISSUES: _____

CARE NOTES: _____

HOME CARE 🏠

Where, When &/or How To

EMERGENCY CONTACT: _____

ROOM:	WIFI:	PASSWORD:	TV/Remote:
TRASH:	CLEANING SUPPLIES:		VACUUM/MOP:
WATER:	COFFEE MAKER:		FURNACE, A/C:
LAUNDRY:			DISHWASHER:
UTILITY SHUTOFFS:			MAIL:

PLANT CARE: _____

OTHER: _____

AFTER NOTES: _____

☆ ☆ ☆ ☆ ☆

MEET-UP:_____

Client

NAME:_____   KEY/CODE:_____

ADDRESS:_____   PHONE:_____

STAY DATES/TIMES:_____

STAY DATES/TIMES:_____

STAY DATES/TIMES:_____

NOTES:_____

🐾 Pet Care

PET:_____	DESC:_____
PET:_____	DESC:_____
PET:_____	DESC:_____
PET:_____	DESC:_____
PET:_____	DESC:_____

FEEDING

PET(S):_____	TIME(S):_____	AMOUNT:_____	FOOD:_____
PET(S):_____	TIME(S):_____	AMOUNT:_____	FOOD:_____
PET(S):_____	TIME(S):_____	AMOUNT:_____	FOOD:_____

MEDICATION

PET:_____	MED:_____	DOSE:_____
PET:_____	MED:_____	DOSE:_____
PET:_____	MED:_____	DOSE:_____
PET:_____	MED:_____	DOSE:_____

WALKS:_____   💩 DISPOSAL:_____

VETERINARIAN:_____

ADDRESS:_____   PHONE:_____

ISSUES:_____

CARE NOTES:_____

HOME CARE 🏠

Where, When &/or How To

EMERGENCY CONTACT:_____

ROOM:_____	WIFI:_____	PASSWORD:_____	TV/Remote:_____
TRASH:_____	CLEANING SUPPLIES:_____		VACUUM/MOP:_____
WATER:_____	COFFEE MAKER:_____		FURNACE, A/C:_____
LAUNDRY:_____			DISHWASHER:_____
UTILITY SHUTOFFS:_____			MAIL:_____

PLANT CARE:_____

OTHER:_____

AFTER NOTES:_____

☆ ☆ ☆ ☆ ☆

Client

NAME: _____ KEY/CODE: _____

ADDRESS: _____ PHONE: _____

STAY DATES/TIMES: _____

STAY DATES/TIMES: _____

STAY DATES/TIMES: _____

NOTES: _____

🐾 Pet Care

PET:	DESC:		
PET:	DESC:		
PET:	DESC:		
PET:	DESC:		
PET:	DESC:		

FEEDING

PET(S):	TIME(S):	AMOUNT:	FOOD:
PET(S):	TIME(S):	AMOUNT:	FOOD:
PET(S):	TIME(S):	AMOUNT:	FOOD:

MEDICATION

PET:	MED:	DOSE:
PET:	MED:	DOSE:
PET:	MED:	DOSE:
PET:	MED:	DOSE:

WALKS: _____ 💩 DISPOSAL: _____

VETERINARIAN: _____

ADDRESS: _____ PHONE: _____

ISSUES: _____

CARE NOTES: _____

HOME CARE 🏠

EMERGENCY CONTACT: _____

Where, When &/or How To

ROOM:	WIFI:	PASSWORD:	TV/Remote:
TRASH:	CLEANING SUPPLIES:		VACUUM/MOP:
WATER:	COFFEE MAKER:		FURNACE, A/C:
LAUNDRY:			DISHWASHER:
UTILITY SHUTOFFS:			MAIL:

PLANT CARE: _____

OTHER: _____

AFTER NOTES: _____

☆ ☆ ☆ ☆ ☆

Client

NAME: KEY/CODE:

ADDRESS: PHONE:

STAY DATES/TIMES:

STAY DATES/TIMES:

STAY DATES/TIMES:

NOTES:

❧ Pet Care

PET: DESC:

PET: DESC:

PET: DESC:

PET: DESC:

PET: DESC:

FEEDING

PET(S):   TIME(S):   AMOUNT: FOOD:

PET(S):   TIME(S):   AMOUNT: FOOD:

PET(S):   TIME(S):   AMOUNT: FOOD:

MEDICATION

PET: MED: DOSE:

PET: MED: DOSE:

PET: MED: DOSE:

PET: MED: DOSE:

WALKS: 💩 DISPOSAL:

VETERINARIAN:

ADDRESS: PHONE:

ISSUES:

CARE NOTES:

HOME CARE 🏠

Where, When &/or How To

EMERGENCY CONTACT:

ROOM: WIFI: PASSWORD: TV/Remote:

TRASH: CLEANING SUPPLIES: VACUUM/MOP:

WATER: COFFEE MAKER: FURNACE, A/C:

LAUNDRY: DISHWASHER:

UTILITY SHUTOFFS: MAIL:

PLANT CARE:

OTHER:

AFTER NOTES:

☆ ☆ ☆ ☆ ☆

Client

MEET-UP: _____

NAME: _____
KEY/CODE: _____

ADDRESS: _____
PHONE: _____

STAY DATES/TIMES: _____

STAY DATES/TIMES: _____

STAY DATES/TIMES: _____

NOTES: _____

☙ Pet Care

PET: _____ DESC: _____

PET: _____ DESC: _____

PET: _____ DESC: _____

PET: _____ DESC: _____

PET: _____ DESC: _____

FEEDING

PET(S): _____ TIME(S): _____ AMOUNT: _____ FOOD: _____

PET(S): _____ TIME(S): _____ AMOUNT: _____ FOOD: _____

PET(S): _____ TIME(S): _____ AMOUNT: _____ FOOD: _____

MEDICATION

PET: _____ MED: _____ DOSE: _____

PET: _____ MED: _____ DOSE: _____

PET: _____ MED: _____ DOSE: _____

PET: _____ MED: _____ DOSE: _____

WALKS: _____ 💩 DISPOSAL: _____

VETERINARIAN: _____

ADDRESS: _____ PHONE: _____

ISSUES: _____

CARE NOTES: _____

HOME CARE ⌂

EMERGENCY CONTACT: _____

Where, When &/or How To

ROOM: _____ WIFI: _____ PASSWORD: _____ TV/Remote: _____

TRASH: _____ CLEANING SUPPLIES: _____ VACUUM/MOP: _____

WATER: _____ COFFEE MAKER: _____ FURNACE, A/C: _____

LAUNDRY: _____ DISHWASHER: _____

UTILITY SHUTOFFS: _____ MAIL: _____

PLANT CARE: _____

OTHER: _____

AFTER NOTES: _____

☆☆☆☆☆

MEET-UP: _____

Client

NAME: _____   KEY/CODE: _____

ADDRESS: _____   PHONE: _____

STAY DATES/TIMES: _____

STAY DATES/TIMES: _____

STAY DATES/TIMES: _____

NOTES: _____

🐾 Pet Care

PET: _____ DESC: _____

PET: _____ DESC: _____

PET: _____ DESC: _____

PET: _____ DESC: _____

PET: _____ DESC: _____

FEEDING

PET(S): _____ TIME(S): _____ AMOUNT: _____ FOOD: _____

PET(S): _____ TIME(S): _____ AMOUNT: _____ FOOD: _____

PET(S): _____ TIME(S): _____ AMOUNT: _____ FOOD: _____

MEDICATION

PET: _____ MED: _____ DOSE: _____

PET: _____ MED: _____ DOSE: _____

PET: _____ MED: _____ DOSE: _____

PET: _____ MED: _____ DOSE: _____

WALKS: _____ 💩 DISPOSAL: _____

VETERINARIAN: _____

ADDRESS: _____ PHONE: _____

ISSUES: _____

CARE NOTES: _____

HOME CARE 🏠

EMERGENCY CONTACT: _____

Where, When &/or How To

ROOM: _____ WIFI: _____ PASSWORD: _____ TV/Remote: _____

TRASH: _____ CLEANING SUPPLIES: _____ VACUUM/MOP: _____

WATER: _____ COFFEE MAKER: _____ FURNACE, A/C: _____

LAUNDRY: _____ DISHWASHER: _____

UTILITY SHUTOFFS: _____ MAIL: _____

PLANT CARE: _____

OTHER: _____

AFTER NOTES: _____

☆ ☆ ☆ ☆ ☆

Client

MEET-UP: _____

NAME: _____ KEY/CODE: _____

ADDRESS: _____ PHONE: _____

STAY DATES/TIMES: _____

STAY DATES/TIMES: _____

STAY DATES/TIMES: _____

NOTES: _____

🐾 Pet Care

PET: _____ DESC: _____

PET: _____ DESC: _____

PET: _____ DESC: _____

PET: _____ DESC: _____

PET: _____ DESC: _____

FEEDING

PET(S): _____ TIME(S): _____ AMOUNT: _____ FOOD: _____

PET(S): _____ TIME(S): _____ AMOUNT: _____ FOOD: _____

PET(S): _____ TIME(S): _____ AMOUNT: _____ FOOD: _____

MEDICATION

PET: _____ MED: _____ DOSE: _____

PET: _____ MED: _____ DOSE: _____

PET: _____ MED: _____ DOSE: _____

PET: _____ MED: _____ DOSE: _____

WALKS: _____ 💩 DISPOSAL: _____

VETERINARIAN: _____

ADDRESS: _____ PHONE: _____

ISSUES: _____

CARE NOTES: _____

HOME CARE 🏠

Where, When &/or How To

EMERGENCY CONTACT: _____

ROOM: _____ WIFI: _____ PASSWORD: _____ TV/Remote: _____

TRASH: _____ CLEANING SUPPLIES: _____ VACUUM/MOP: _____

WATER: _____ COFFEE MAKER: _____ FURNACE, A/C: _____

LAUNDRY: _____ DISHWASHER: _____

UTILITY SHUTOFFS: _____ MAIL: _____

PLANT CARE: _____

OTHER: _____

AFTER NOTES: _____

☆ ☆ ☆ ☆ ☆

MEET-UP: _____

Client

NAME: _____ KEY/CODE: _____

ADDRESS: _____ PHONE: _____

STAY DATES/TIMES: _____

STAY DATES/TIMES: _____

STAY DATES/TIMES: _____

NOTES: _____

🐾 Pet Care

PET: _____ DESC: _____

PET: _____ DESC: _____

PET: _____ DESC: _____

PET: _____ DESC: _____

PET: _____ DESC: _____

FEEDING

PET(S): _____ TIME(S): _____ AMOUNT: _____ FOOD: _____

PET(S): _____ TIME(S): _____ AMOUNT: _____ FOOD: _____

PET(S): _____ TIME(S): _____ AMOUNT: _____ FOOD: _____

MEDICATION

PET: _____ MED: _____ DOSE: _____

PET: _____ MED: _____ DOSE: _____

PET: _____ MED: _____ DOSE: _____

PET: _____ MED: _____ DOSE: _____

WALKS: _____ 💩 DISPOSAL: _____

VETERINARIAN: _____

ADDRESS: _____ PHONE: _____

ISSUES: _____

CARE NOTES: _____

HOME CARE 🏠

Where, When &/or How To

EMERGENCY CONTACT: _____

ROOM: _____ WIFI: _____ PASSWORD: _____ TV/Remote: _____

TRASH: _____ CLEANING SUPPLIES: _____ VACUUM/MOP: _____

WATER: _____ COFFEE MAKER: _____ FURNACE, A/C: _____

LAUNDRY: _____ DISHWASHER: _____

UTILITY SHUTOFFS: _____ MAIL: _____

PLANT CARE: _____

OTHER: _____

AFTER NOTES: _____

☆ ☆ ☆ ☆ ☆

Client

NAME: _____   KEY/CODE: _____

ADDRESS: _____   PHONE: _____

STAY DATES/TIMES: _____

STAY DATES/TIMES: _____

STAY DATES/TIMES: _____

NOTES: _____

🐾 Pet Care

PET: _____ DESC: _____

PET: _____ DESC: _____

PET: _____ DESC: _____

PET: _____ DESC: _____

PET: _____ DESC: _____

FEEDING

PET(S): _____ TIME(S): _____ AMOUNT: _____ FOOD: _____

PET(S): _____ TIME(S): _____ AMOUNT: _____ FOOD: _____

PET(S): _____ TIME(S): _____ AMOUNT: _____ FOOD: _____

MEDICATION

PET: _____ MED: _____ DOSE: _____

PET: _____ MED: _____ DOSE: _____

PET: _____ MED: _____ DOSE: _____

PET: _____ MED: _____ DOSE: _____

WALKS: _____ 💩 DISPOSAL: _____

VETERINARIAN: _____

ADDRESS: _____ PHONE: _____

ISSUES: _____

CARE NOTES: _____

HOME CARE 🏠

EMERGENCY CONTACT: _____

Where, When &/or How To

ROOM: _____ WIFI: _____ PASSWORD: _____ TV/Remote: _____

TRASH: _____ CLEANING SUPPLIES: _____ VACUUM/MOP: _____

WATER: _____ COFFEE MAKER: _____ FURNACE, A/C: _____

LAUNDRY: _____ DISHWASHER: _____

UTILITY SHUTOFFS: _____ MAIL: _____

PLANT CARE: _____

OTHER: _____

AFTER NOTES: _____

☆ ☆ ☆ ☆ ☆

MEET-UP: _____

Client

NAME: _____ KEY/CODE: _____

ADDRESS: _____ PHONE: _____

STAY DATES/TIMES: _____

STAY DATES/TIMES: _____

STAY DATES/TIMES: _____

NOTES: _____

🐾 Pet Care

PET: _____ DESC: _____

PET: _____ DESC: _____

PET: _____ DESC: _____

PET: _____ DESC: _____

PET: _____ DESC: _____

FEEDING

PET(S): _____ TIME(S): _____ AMOUNT: _____ FOOD: _____

PET(S): _____ TIME(S): _____ AMOUNT: _____ FOOD: _____

PET(S): _____ TIME(S): _____ AMOUNT: _____ FOOD: _____

MEDICATION

PET: _____ MED: _____ DOSE: _____

PET: _____ MED: _____ DOSE: _____

PET: _____ MED: _____ DOSE: _____

PET: _____ MED: _____ DOSE: _____

WALKS: _____ 💩 DISPOSAL: _____

VETERINARIAN: _____

ADDRESS: _____ PHONE: _____

ISSUES: _____

CARE NOTES: _____

HOME CARE 🏠

Where, When &/or How To

EMERGENCY CONTACT: _____

ROOM: _____ WIFI: _____ PASSWORD: _____ TV/Remote: _____

TRASH: _____ CLEANING SUPPLIES: _____ VACUUM/MOP: _____

WATER: _____ COFFEE MAKER: _____ FURNACE, A/C: _____

LAUNDRY: _____ DISHWASHER: _____

UTILITY SHUTOFFS: _____ MAIL: _____

PLANT CARE: _____

OTHER: _____

AFTER NOTES: _____

☆ ☆ ☆ ☆ ☆

Client

NAME: _____ KEY/CODE: _____

ADDRESS: _____ PHONE: _____

STAY DATES/TIMES: _____

STAY DATES/TIMES: _____

STAY DATES/TIMES: _____

NOTES: _____

❀ Pet Care

PET: _____ DESC: _____

PET: _____ DESC: _____

PET: _____ DESC: _____

PET: _____ DESC: _____

PET: _____ DESC: _____

	PET(S):	TIME(S):	AMOUNT:	FOOD:
FEEDING	PET(S):	TIME(S):	AMOUNT:	FOOD:
	PET(S):	TIME(S):	AMOUNT:	FOOD:

	PET:	MED:	DOSE:
MEDICATION	PET:	MED:	DOSE:
	PET:	MED:	DOSE:
	PET:	MED:	DOSE:

WALKS: _____ 💩 DISPOSAL: _____

VETERINARIAN: _____

ADDRESS: _____ PHONE: _____

ISSUES: _____

CARE NOTES: _____

HOME CARE 🏠

EMERGENCY CONTACT: _____

	ROOM:	WIFI:	PASSWORD:	TV/Remote:
Where, When &/or How To	TRASH:	CLEANING SUPPLIES:		VACUUM/MOP:
	WATER:	COFFEE MAKER:		FURNACE, A/C:
	LAUNDRY:			DISHWASHER:
	UTILITY SHUTOFFS:			MAIL:
	PLANT CARE:			

OTHER: _____

AFTER NOTES: _____

☆ ☆ ☆ ☆ ☆

MEET-UP: _____

Client

NAME: _____   KEY/CODE: _____

ADDRESS: _____   PHONE: _____

STAY DATES/TIMES: _____

STAY DATES/TIMES: _____

STAY DATES/TIMES: _____

NOTES: _____

🐾 Pet Care

PET: _____ DESC: _____

PET: _____ DESC: _____

PET: _____ DESC: _____

PET: _____ DESC: _____

PET: _____ DESC: _____

FEEDING

PET(S): _____ TIME(S): _____ AMOUNT: _____ FOOD: _____

PET(S): _____ TIME(S): _____ AMOUNT: _____ FOOD: _____

PET(S): _____ TIME(S): _____ AMOUNT: _____ FOOD: _____

MEDICATION

PET: _____ MED: _____ DOSE: _____

PET: _____ MED: _____ DOSE: _____

PET: _____ MED: _____ DOSE: _____

PET: _____ MED: _____ DOSE: _____

WALKS: _____   💩 DISPOSAL: _____

VETERINARIAN: _____

ADDRESS: _____ PHONE: _____

ISSUES: _____

CARE NOTES: _____

HOME CARE 🏠

EMERGENCY CONTACT: _____

Where, When &/or How To

ROOM: _____ WIFI: _____ PASSWORD: _____ TV/Remote: _____

TRASH: _____ CLEANING SUPPLIES: _____ VACUUM/MOP: _____

WATER: _____ COFFEE MAKER: _____ FURNACE, A/C: _____

LAUNDRY: _____ DISHWASHER: _____

UTILITY SHUTOFFS: _____ MAIL: _____

PLANT CARE: _____

OTHER: _____

AFTER NOTES: _____

☆ ☆ ☆ ☆ ☆

Client

MEET-UP: _____

NAME: _____   KEY/CODE: _____

ADDRESS: _____   PHONE: _____

STAY DATES/TIMES: _____

STAY DATES/TIMES: _____

STAY DATES/TIMES: _____

NOTES: _____

☙ Pet Care

PET: _____ DESC: _____

PET: _____ DESC: _____

PET: _____ DESC: _____

PET: _____ DESC: _____

PET: _____ DESC: _____

FEEDING

PET(S): _____ TIME(S): _____ AMOUNT: _____ FOOD: _____

PET(S): _____ TIME(S): _____ AMOUNT: _____ FOOD: _____

PET(S): _____ TIME(S): _____ AMOUNT: _____ FOOD: _____

MEDICATION

PET: _____ MED: _____ DOSE: _____

PET: _____ MED: _____ DOSE: _____

PET: _____ MED: _____ DOSE: _____

PET: _____ MED: _____ DOSE: _____

WALKS: _____ 💩 DISPOSAL: _____

VETERINARIAN: _____

ADDRESS: _____ PHONE: _____

ISSUES: _____

CARE NOTES: _____

HOME CARE 🏠

EMERGENCY CONTACT: _____

Where, When &/or How To

ROOM: _____ WIFI: _____ PASSWORD: _____ TV/Remote: _____

TRASH: _____ CLEANING SUPPLIES: _____ VACUUM/MOP: _____

WATER: _____ COFFEE MAKER: _____ FURNACE, A/C: _____

LAUNDRY: _____ DISHWASHER: _____

UTILITY SHUTOFFS: _____ MAIL: _____

PLANT CARE: _____

OTHER: _____

AFTER NOTES: _____

☆ ☆ ☆ ☆ ☆

MEET-UP: _____

Client

NAME: _____ KEY/CODE: _____

ADDRESS: _____ PHONE: _____

STAY DATES/TIMES: _____

STAY DATES/TIMES: _____

STAY DATES/TIMES: _____

NOTES: _____

☸ Pet Care

PET:	DESC:	
PET:	DESC:	
PET:	DESC:	
PET:	DESC:	
PET:	DESC:	

FEEDING

PET(S):	TIME(S):	AMOUNT:	FOOD:
PET(S):	TIME(S):	AMOUNT:	FOOD:
PET(S):	TIME(S):	AMOUNT:	FOOD:

MEDICATION

PET:	MED:	DOSE:
PET:	MED:	DOSE:
PET:	MED:	DOSE:
PET:	MED:	DOSE:

WALKS: _____ 💩 DISPOSAL: _____

VETERINARIAN: _____

ADDRESS: _____ PHONE: _____

ISSUES: _____

CARE NOTES: _____

HOME CARE ⌂

Where, When &/or How To

EMERGENCY CONTACT: _____

ROOM:	WIFI:	PASSWORD:	TV/Remote:
TRASH:	CLEANING SUPPLIES:		VACUUM/MOP:
WATER:	COFFEE MAKER:		FURNACE, A/C:
LAUNDRY:			DISHWASHER:
UTILITY SHUTOFFS:			MAIL:

PLANT CARE: _____

OTHER: _____

AFTER NOTES: _____

☆☆☆☆☆

Client

MEET-UP: _____

NAME: _____ KEY/CODE: _____

ADDRESS: _____ PHONE: _____

STAY DATES/TIMES: _____

STAY DATES/TIMES: _____

STAY DATES/TIMES: _____

NOTES: _____

🐾 Pet Care

PET: _____ DESC: _____

PET: _____ DESC: _____

PET: _____ DESC: _____

PET: _____ DESC: _____

PET: _____ DESC: _____

FEEDING

PET(S): _____ TIME(S): _____ AMOUNT: _____ FOOD: _____

PET(S): _____ TIME(S): _____ AMOUNT: _____ FOOD: _____

PET(S): _____ TIME(S): _____ AMOUNT: _____ FOOD: _____

MEDICATION

PET: _____ MED: _____ DOSE: _____

PET: _____ MED: _____ DOSE: _____

PET: _____ MED: _____ DOSE: _____

PET: _____ MED: _____ DOSE: _____

WALKS: _____ 💩 DISPOSAL: _____

VETERINARIAN: _____

ADDRESS: _____ PHONE: _____

ISSUES: _____

CARE NOTES: _____

HOME CARE 🏠

EMERGENCY CONTACT: _____

Where, When &/or How To

ROOM: _____ WIFI: _____ PASSWORD: _____ TV/Remote: _____

TRASH: _____ CLEANING SUPPLIES: _____ VACUUM/MOP: _____

WATER: _____ COFFEE MAKER: _____ FURNACE, A/C: _____

LAUNDRY: _____ DISHWASHER: _____

UTILITY SHUTOFFS: _____ MAIL: _____

PLANT CARE: _____

OTHER: _____

AFTER NOTES: _____

☆ ☆ ☆ ☆ ☆

Client

NAME: _____ KEY/CODE: _____

ADDRESS: _____ PHONE: _____

STAY DATES/TIMES: _____

STAY DATES/TIMES: _____

STAY DATES/TIMES: _____

NOTES: _____

☙ Pet Care

PET: _____ DESC: _____

PET: _____ DESC: _____

PET: _____ DESC: _____

PET: _____ DESC: _____

PET: _____ DESC: _____

FEEDING

PET(S): _____ TIME(S): _____ AMOUNT: _____ FOOD: _____

PET(S): _____ TIME(S): _____ AMOUNT: _____ FOOD: _____

PET(S): _____ TIME(S): _____ AMOUNT: _____ FOOD: _____

MEDICATION

PET: _____ MED: _____ DOSE: _____

PET: _____ MED: _____ DOSE: _____

PET: _____ MED: _____ DOSE: _____

PET: _____ MED: _____ DOSE: _____

WALKS: _____ 💩 DISPOSAL: _____

VETERINARIAN: _____

ADDRESS: _____ PHONE: _____

ISSUES: _____

CARE NOTES: _____

HOME CARE ⌂

EMERGENCY CONTACT: _____

Where, When &/or How To

ROOM: _____ WIFI: _____ PASSWORD: _____ TV/Remote: _____

TRASH: _____ CLEANING SUPPLIES: _____ VACUUM/MOP: _____

WATER: _____ COFFEE MAKER: _____ FURNACE, A/C: _____

LAUNDRY: _____ DISHWASHER: _____

UTILITY SHUTOFFS: _____ MAIL: _____

PLANT CARE: _____

OTHER: _____

AFTER NOTES: _____

☆ ☆ ☆ ☆ ☆

Client

MEET-UP:_____

NAME:

KEY/CODE:

ADDRESS:

PHONE:

STAY DATES/TIMES:

STAY DATES/TIMES:

STAY DATES/TIMES:

NOTES:

🐾 Pet Care

PET: DESC:

PET: DESC:

PET: DESC:

PET: DESC:

PET: DESC:

FEEDING

PET(S):   TIME(S):   AMOUNT: FOOD:

PET(S):   TIME(S):   AMOUNT: FOOD:

PET(S):   TIME(S):   AMOUNT: FOOD:

MEDICATION

PET: MED: DOSE:

PET: MED: DOSE:

PET: MED: DOSE:

PET: MED: DOSE:

WALKS: 💩 DISPOSAL:

VETERINARIAN:

ADDRESS: PHONE:

ISSUES:

CARE NOTES:

HOME CARE 🏠

Where, When &/or How To

EMERGENCY CONTACT:

ROOM: WIFI: PASSWORD: TV/Remote:

TRASH: CLEANING SUPPLIES: VACUUM/MOP:

WATER: COFFEE MAKER: FURNACE, A/C:

LAUNDRY: DISHWASHER:

UTILITY SHUTOFFS: MAIL:

PLANT CARE:

OTHER:

AFTER NOTES:

☆ ☆ ☆ ☆ ☆

MEET-UP: _____   # Client

NAME: _____   KEY/CODE: _____

ADDRESS: _____   PHONE: _____

STAY DATES/TIMES: _____

STAY DATES/TIMES: _____

STAY DATES/TIMES: _____

NOTES: _____

🐾 Pet Care

PET: _____	DESC: _____		
PET: _____	DESC: _____		
PET: _____	DESC: _____		
PET: _____	DESC: _____		
PET: _____	DESC: _____		

FEEDING

PET(S): _____	TIME(S): _____	AMOUNT: _____	FOOD: _____
PET(S): _____	TIME(S): _____	AMOUNT: _____	FOOD: _____
PET(S): _____	TIME(S): _____	AMOUNT: _____	FOOD: _____

MEDICATION

PET: _____	MED: _____	DOSE: _____
PET: _____	MED: _____	DOSE: _____
PET: _____	MED: _____	DOSE: _____
PET: _____	MED: _____	DOSE: _____

WALKS: _____   💩 DISPOSAL: _____

VETERINARIAN: _____

ADDRESS: _____   PHONE: _____

ISSUES: _____

CARE NOTES: _____

HOME CARE 🏠

EMERGENCY CONTACT: _____

Where, When &/or How To

ROOM: _____	WIFI: _____	PASSWORD: _____	TV/Remote: _____
TRASH: _____	CLEANING SUPPLIES: _____		VACUUM/MOP: _____
WATER: _____	COFFEE MAKER: _____		FURNACE, A/C: _____
LAUNDRY: _____			DISHWASHER: _____
UTILITY SHUTOFFS: _____			MAIL: _____

PLANT CARE: _____

OTHER: _____

AFTER NOTES: _____

☆ ☆ ☆ ☆ ☆

Client

NAME: _____ KEY/CODE: _____

ADDRESS: _____ PHONE: _____

STAY DATES/TIMES: _____

STAY DATES/TIMES: _____

STAY DATES/TIMES: _____

NOTES: _____

🐾 Pet Care

PET: _____ DESC: _____

PET: _____ DESC: _____

PET: _____ DESC: _____

PET: _____ DESC: _____

PET: _____ DESC: _____

PET(S):	TIME(S):	AMOUNT:	FOOD:
PET(S):	TIME(S):	AMOUNT:	FOOD:
PET(S):	TIME(S):	AMOUNT:	FOOD:

FEEDING

PET:	MED:	DOSE:
PET:	MED:	DOSE:
PET:	MED:	DOSE:
PET:	MED:	DOSE:

MEDICATION

WALKS: _____ 💩 DISPOSAL: _____

VETERINARIAN: _____

ADDRESS: _____ PHONE: _____

ISSUES: _____

CARE NOTES: _____

HOME CARE 🏠

EMERGENCY CONTACT: _____

ROOM: _____ WIFI: _____ PASSWORD: _____ TV/Remote: _____

TRASH: _____ CLEANING SUPPLIES: _____ VACUUM/MOP: _____

WATER: _____ COFFEE MAKER: _____ FURNACE, A/C: _____

LAUNDRY: _____ DISHWASHER: _____

UTILITY SHUTOFFS: _____ MAIL: _____

PLANT CARE: _____

OTHER: _____

Where, When &/or How To

AFTER NOTES: _____

☆ ☆ ☆ ☆ ☆

MEET-UP: _____

Client

NAME: _____ KEY/CODE: _____

ADDRESS: _____ PHONE: _____

STAY DATES/TIMES: _____

STAY DATES/TIMES: _____

STAY DATES/TIMES: _____

NOTES: _____

🐾 Pet Care

PET: _____ DESC: _____

PET: _____ DESC: _____

PET: _____ DESC: _____

PET: _____ DESC: _____

PET: _____ DESC: _____

FEEDING

PET(S): _____ TIME(S): _____ AMOUNT: _____ FOOD: _____

PET(S): _____ TIME(S): _____ AMOUNT: _____ FOOD: _____

PET(S): _____ TIME(S): _____ AMOUNT: _____ FOOD: _____

MEDICATION

PET: _____ MED: _____ DOSE: _____

PET: _____ MED: _____ DOSE: _____

PET: _____ MED: _____ DOSE: _____

PET: _____ MED: _____ DOSE: _____

WALKS: _____ 💩 DISPOSAL: _____

VETERINARIAN: _____

ADDRESS: _____ PHONE: _____

ISSUES: _____

CARE NOTES: _____

HOME CARE 🏠

Where, When &/or How To

EMERGENCY CONTACT: _____

ROOM: _____ WIFI: _____ PASSWORD: _____ TV/Remote: _____

TRASH: _____ CLEANING SUPPLIES: _____ VACUUM/MOP: _____

WATER: _____ COFFEE MAKER: _____ FURNACE, A/C: _____

LAUNDRY: _____ DISHWASHER: _____

UTILITY SHUTOFFS: _____ MAIL: _____

PLANT CARE: _____

OTHER: _____

AFTER NOTES: _____

☆ ☆ ☆ ☆ ☆

Client

MEET-UP: _____

NAME: _____   KEY/CODE: _____

ADDRESS: _____   PHONE: _____

STAY DATES/TIMES: _____

STAY DATES/TIMES: _____

STAY DATES/TIMES: _____

NOTES: _____

🐾 Pet Care

PET: _____ DESC: _____

PET: _____ DESC: _____

PET: _____ DESC: _____

PET: _____ DESC: _____

PET: _____ DESC: _____

FEEDING

PET(S): _____ TIME(S): _____ AMOUNT: _____ FOOD: _____

PET(S): _____ TIME(S): _____ AMOUNT: _____ FOOD: _____

PET(S): _____ TIME(S): _____ AMOUNT: _____ FOOD: _____

MEDICATION

PET: _____ MED: _____ DOSE: _____

PET: _____ MED: _____ DOSE: _____

PET: _____ MED: _____ DOSE: _____

PET: _____ MED: _____ DOSE: _____

WALKS: _____   💩 DISPOSAL: _____

VETERINARIAN: _____

ADDRESS: _____   PHONE: _____

ISSUES: _____

CARE NOTES: _____

HOME CARE 🏠

Where, When &/or How To

EMERGENCY CONTACT: _____

ROOM: _____ WIFI: _____ PASSWORD: _____ TV/Remote: _____

TRASH: _____ CLEANING SUPPLIES: _____ VACUUM/MOP: _____

WATER: _____ COFFEE MAKER: _____ FURNACE, A/C: _____

LAUNDRY: _____ DISHWASHER: _____

UTILITY SHUTOFFS: _____ MAIL: _____

PLANT CARE: _____

OTHER: _____

AFTER NOTES: _____

☆ ☆ ☆ ☆ ☆

MEET-UP: _____

Client

NAME: _____   KEY/CODE: _____

ADDRESS: _____   PHONE: _____

STAY DATES/TIMES: _____

STAY DATES/TIMES: _____

STAY DATES/TIMES: _____

NOTES: _____

🐾 Pet Care

PET: _____ DESC: _____

PET: _____ DESC: _____

PET: _____ DESC: _____

PET: _____ DESC: _____

PET: _____ DESC: _____

FEEDING

PET(S): _____ TIME(S): _____ AMOUNT: _____ FOOD: _____

PET(S): _____ TIME(S): _____ AMOUNT: _____ FOOD: _____

PET(S): _____ TIME(S): _____ AMOUNT: _____ FOOD: _____

MEDICATION

PET: _____ MED: _____ DOSE: _____

PET: _____ MED: _____ DOSE: _____

PET: _____ MED: _____ DOSE: _____

PET: _____ MED: _____ DOSE: _____

WALKS: _____ 💩 DISPOSAL: _____

VETERINARIAN: _____

ADDRESS: _____ PHONE: _____

ISSUES: _____

CARE NOTES: _____

HOME CARE 🏠

EMERGENCY CONTACT: _____

Where, When &/or How To

ROOM: _____ WIFI: _____ PASSWORD: _____ TV/Remote: _____

TRASH: _____ CLEANING SUPPLIES: _____ VACUUM/MOP: _____

WATER: _____ COFFEE MAKER: _____ FURNACE, A/C: _____

LAUNDRY: _____ DISHWASHER: _____

UTILITY SHUTOFFS: _____ MAIL: _____

PLANT CARE: _____

OTHER: _____

AFTER NOTES: _____

☆ ☆ ☆ ☆ ☆

Client

MEET-UP: _____

NAME: _____ KEY/CODE: _____

ADDRESS: _____ PHONE: _____

STAY DATES/TIMES: _____

STAY DATES/TIMES: _____

STAY DATES/TIMES: _____

NOTES: _____

🐾 Pet Care

PET: _____ DESC: _____

PET: _____ DESC: _____

PET: _____ DESC: _____

PET: _____ DESC: _____

PET: _____ DESC: _____

FEEDING

PET(S): _____ TIME(S): _____ AMOUNT: _____ FOOD: _____

PET(S): _____ TIME(S): _____ AMOUNT: _____ FOOD: _____

PET(S): _____ TIME(S): _____ AMOUNT: _____ FOOD: _____

MEDICATION

PET: _____ MED: _____ DOSE: _____

PET: _____ MED: _____ DOSE: _____

PET: _____ MED: _____ DOSE: _____

PET: _____ MED: _____ DOSE: _____

WALKS: _____ 💩 DISPOSAL: _____

VETERINARIAN: _____

ADDRESS: _____ PHONE: _____

ISSUES: _____

CARE NOTES: _____

HOME CARE 🏠

Where, When &/or How To

EMERGENCY CONTACT: _____

ROOM: _____ WIFI: _____ PASSWORD: _____ TV/Remote: _____

TRASH: _____ CLEANING SUPPLIES: _____ VACUUM/MOP: _____

WATER: _____ COFFEE MAKER: _____ FURNACE, A/C: _____

LAUNDRY: _____ DISHWASHER: _____

UTILITY SHUTOFFS: _____ MAIL: _____

PLANT CARE: _____

_____

OTHER: _____

AFTER NOTES: _____

☆ ☆ ☆ ☆ ☆

Client

NAME: _____ KEY/CODE: _____

ADDRESS: _____ PHONE: _____

STAY DATES/TIMES: _____

STAY DATES/TIMES: _____

STAY DATES/TIMES: _____

NOTES: _____

✿ Pet Care

PET: _____ DESC: _____

PET: _____ DESC: _____

PET: _____ DESC: _____

PET: _____ DESC: _____

PET: _____ DESC: _____

FEEDING

PET(S): _____ TIME(S): _____ AMOUNT: _____ FOOD: _____

PET(S): _____ TIME(S): _____ AMOUNT: _____ FOOD: _____

PET(S): _____ TIME(S): _____ AMOUNT: _____ FOOD: _____

MEDICATION

PET: _____ MED: _____ DOSE: _____

PET: _____ MED: _____ DOSE: _____

PET: _____ MED: _____ DOSE: _____

PET: _____ MED: _____ DOSE: _____

WALKS: _____ 💩 DISPOSAL: _____

VETERINARIAN: _____

ADDRESS: _____ PHONE: _____

ISSUES: _____

CARE NOTES: _____

HOME CARE ⌂

EMERGENCY CONTACT: _____

Where, When &/or How To

ROOM: _____ WIFI: _____ PASSWORD: _____ TV/Remote: _____

TRASH: _____ CLEANING SUPPLIES: _____ VACUUM/MOP: _____

WATER: _____ COFFEE MAKER: _____ FURNACE, A/C: _____

LAUNDRY: _____ DISHWASHER: _____

UTILITY SHUTOFFS: _____ MAIL: _____

PLANT CARE: _____

OTHER: _____

AFTER NOTES: _____

☆ ☆ ☆ ☆ ☆

Client

MEET-UP: _____

NAME: _____   KEY/CODE: _____

ADDRESS: _____   PHONE: _____

STAY DATES/TIMES: _____

STAY DATES/TIMES: _____

STAY DATES/TIMES: _____

NOTES: _____

🐾 Pet Care

PET: _____ DESC: _____

PET: _____ DESC: _____

PET: _____ DESC: _____

PET: _____ DESC: _____

PET: _____ DESC: _____

FEEDING

PET(S): _____ TIME(S): _____ AMOUNT: _____ FOOD: _____

PET(S): _____ TIME(S): _____ AMOUNT: _____ FOOD: _____

PET(S): _____ TIME(S): _____ AMOUNT: _____ FOOD: _____

MEDICATION

PET: _____ MED: _____ DOSE: _____

PET: _____ MED: _____ DOSE: _____

PET: _____ MED: _____ DOSE: _____

PET: _____ MED: _____ DOSE: _____

WALKS: _____ 💩 DISPOSAL: _____

VETERINARIAN: _____

ADDRESS: _____ PHONE: _____

ISSUES: _____

CARE NOTES: _____

HOME CARE 🏠

Where, When &/or How To

EMERGENCY CONTACT: _____

ROOM: _____ WIFI: _____ PASSWORD: _____ TV/Remote: _____

TRASH: _____ CLEANING SUPPLIES: _____ VACUUM/MOP: _____

WATER: _____ COFFEE MAKER: _____ FURNACE, A/C: _____

LAUNDRY: _____ DISHWASHER: _____

UTILITY SHUTOFFS: _____ MAIL: _____

PLANT CARE: _____

OTHER: _____

AFTER NOTES: _____

☆ ☆ ☆ ☆ ☆

MEET-UP: _____

Client

NAME: _____   KEY/CODE: _____

ADDRESS: _____   PHONE: _____

STAY DATES/TIMES: _____

STAY DATES/TIMES: _____

STAY DATES/TIMES: _____

NOTES: _____

🐾 Pet Care

PET: _____ DESC: _____

PET: _____ DESC: _____

PET: _____ DESC: _____

PET: _____ DESC: _____

PET: _____ DESC: _____

FEEDING			
PET(S):	TIME(S):	AMOUNT:	FOOD:
PET(S):	TIME(S):	AMOUNT:	FOOD:
PET(S):	TIME(S):	AMOUNT:	FOOD:

MEDICATION		
PET:	MED:	DOSE:
PET:	MED:	DOSE:
PET:	MED:	DOSE:
PET:	MED:	DOSE:

WALKS: _____ 💩 DISPOSAL: _____

VETERINARIAN: _____

ADDRESS: _____ PHONE: _____

ISSUES: _____

CARE NOTES: _____

HOME CARE 🏠

EMERGENCY CONTACT: _____

Where, When &/or How To

ROOM: _____ WIFI: _____ PASSWORD: _____ TV/Remote: _____

TRASH: _____ CLEANING SUPPLIES: _____ VACUUM/MOP: _____

WATER: _____ COFFEE MAKER: _____ FURNACE, A/C: _____

LAUNDRY: _____ DISHWASHER: _____

UTILITY SHUTOFFS: _____ MAIL: _____

PLANT CARE: _____

OTHER: _____

AFTER NOTES: _____

☆ ☆ ☆ ☆ ☆

Client

NAME:

KEY/CODE:

ADDRESS:

PHONE:

STAY DATES/TIMES:

STAY DATES/TIMES:

STAY DATES/TIMES:

NOTES:

❀ Pet Care

PET: DESC:

PET: DESC:

PET: DESC:

PET: DESC:

PET: DESC:

PET(S):   TIME(S):   AMOUNT: FOOD:

PET(S):   TIME(S):   AMOUNT: FOOD:

PET(S):   TIME(S):   AMOUNT: FOOD:

PET: MED: DOSE:

PET: MED: DOSE:

PET: MED: DOSE:

PET: MED: DOSE:

WALKS: 💩 DISPOSAL:

VETERINARIAN:

ADDRESS: PHONE:

ISSUES:

CARE NOTES:

FEEDING *MEDICATION* (sidebar labels)

HOME CARE 🏠

EMERGENCY CONTACT:

ROOM: WIFI: PASSWORD: TV/Remote:

TRASH: CLEANING SUPPLIES: VACUUM/MOP:

WATER: COFFEE MAKER: FURNACE, A/C:

LAUNDRY: DISHWASHER:

UTILITY SHUTOFFS: MAIL:

PLANT CARE:

OTHER:

Where, When &/or How To (sidebar label)

AFTER NOTES:

☆ ☆ ☆ ☆ ☆

MEET-UP: _____

Client

NAME: _____ KEY/CODE: _____

ADDRESS: _____ PHONE: _____

STAY DATES/TIMES: _____

STAY DATES/TIMES: _____

STAY DATES/TIMES: _____

NOTES: _____

☙ Pet Care

PET: _____ DESC: _____

PET: _____ DESC: _____

PET: _____ DESC: _____

PET: _____ DESC: _____

PET: _____ DESC: _____

FEEDING

PET(S): _____ TIME(S): _____ AMOUNT: _____ FOOD: _____

PET(S): _____ TIME(S): _____ AMOUNT: _____ FOOD: _____

PET(S): _____ TIME(S): _____ AMOUNT: _____ FOOD: _____

MEDICATION

PET: _____ MED: _____ DOSE: _____

PET: _____ MED: _____ DOSE: _____

PET: _____ MED: _____ DOSE: _____

PET: _____ MED: _____ DOSE: _____

WALKS: _____ 💩 DISPOSAL: _____

VETERINARIAN: _____

ADDRESS: _____ PHONE: _____

ISSUES: _____

CARE NOTES: _____

HOME CARE 🏠

Where, When &/or How To

EMERGENCY CONTACT: _____

ROOM: _____ WIFI: _____ PASSWORD: _____ TV/Remote: _____

TRASH: _____ CLEANING SUPPLIES: _____ VACUUM/MOP: _____

WATER: _____ COFFEE MAKER: _____ FURNACE, A/C: _____

LAUNDRY: _____ DISHWASHER: _____

UTILITY SHUTOFFS: _____ MAIL: _____

PLANT CARE: _____

OTHER: _____

AFTER NOTES: _____

☆ ☆ ☆ ☆ ☆

Client

MEET-UP: _____

NAME: _____ KEY/CODE: _____

ADDRESS: _____ PHONE: _____

STAY DATES/TIMES: _____

STAY DATES/TIMES: _____

STAY DATES/TIMES: _____

NOTES: _____

🐾 Pet Care

PET: _____ DESC: _____

PET: _____ DESC: _____

PET: _____ DESC: _____

PET: _____ DESC: _____

PET: _____ DESC: _____

FEEDING

PET(S): _____ TIME(S): _____ AMOUNT: _____ FOOD: _____

PET(S): _____ TIME(S): _____ AMOUNT: _____ FOOD: _____

PET(S): _____ TIME(S): _____ AMOUNT: _____ FOOD: _____

MEDICATION

PET: _____ MED: _____ DOSE: _____

PET: _____ MED: _____ DOSE: _____

PET: _____ MED: _____ DOSE: _____

PET: _____ MED: _____ DOSE: _____

WALKS: _____ 💩 DISPOSAL: _____

VETERINARIAN: _____

ADDRESS: _____ PHONE: _____

ISSUES: _____

CARE NOTES: _____

HOME CARE 🏠

Where, When &/or How To

EMERGENCY CONTACT: _____

ROOM: _____ WIFI: _____ PASSWORD: _____ TV/Remote: _____

TRASH: _____ CLEANING SUPPLIES: _____ VACUUM/MOP: _____

WATER: _____ COFFEE MAKER: _____ FURNACE, A/C: _____

LAUNDRY: _____ DISHWASHER: _____

UTILITY SHUTOFFS: _____ MAIL: _____

PLANT CARE: _____

OTHER: _____

AFTER NOTES: _____

☆ ☆ ☆ ☆ ☆

MEET-UP: _____

Client

NAME: _____ KEY/CODE: _____

ADDRESS: _____ PHONE: _____

STAY DATES/TIMES: _____

STAY DATES/TIMES: _____

STAY DATES/TIMES: _____

NOTES: _____

🐾 Pet Care

PET:	DESC:
PET:	DESC:
PET:	DESC:
PET:	DESC:
PET:	DESC:

	PET(S):	TIME(S):	AMOUNT:	FOOD:
FEEDING	PET(S):	TIME(S):	AMOUNT:	FOOD:
	PET(S):	TIME(S):	AMOUNT:	FOOD:

	PET:	MED:	DOSE:
MEDICATION	PET:	MED:	DOSE:
	PET:	MED:	DOSE:
	PET:	MED:	DOSE:

WALKS: _____   💩 DISPOSAL: _____

VETERINARIAN: _____

ADDRESS: _____ PHONE: _____

ISSUES: _____

CARE NOTES: _____

HOME CARE 🏠

EMERGENCY CONTACT: _____

	ROOM:	WIFI:	PASSWORD:	TV/Remote:
	TRASH:	CLEANING SUPPLIES:		VACUUM/MOP:
Where, When &/or How To	WATER:	COFFEE MAKER:		FURNACE, A/C:
	LAUNDRY:			DISHWASHER:
	UTILITY SHUTOFFS:			MAIL:
	PLANT CARE:			

OTHER: _____

AFTER NOTES: _____

☆ ☆ ☆ ☆ ☆

Client

MEET-UP: _____

NAME: _____ KEY/CODE: _____

ADDRESS: _____ PHONE: _____

STAY DATES/TIMES: _____

STAY DATES/TIMES: _____

STAY DATES/TIMES: _____

NOTES: _____

🐾 Pet Care

PET: _____ DESC: _____

PET: _____ DESC: _____

PET: _____ DESC: _____

PET: _____ DESC: _____

PET: _____ DESC: _____

FEEDING

PET(S): _____ TIME(S): _____ AMOUNT: _____ FOOD: _____

PET(S): _____ TIME(S): _____ AMOUNT: _____ FOOD: _____

PET(S): _____ TIME(S): _____ AMOUNT: _____ FOOD: _____

MEDICATION

PET: _____ MED: _____ DOSE: _____

PET: _____ MED: _____ DOSE: _____

PET: _____ MED: _____ DOSE: _____

PET: _____ MED: _____ DOSE: _____

WALKS: _____ 💩 DISPOSAL: _____

VETERINARIAN: _____

ADDRESS: _____ PHONE: _____

ISSUES: _____

CARE NOTES: _____

HOME CARE 🏠

Where, When &/or How To

EMERGENCY CONTACT: _____

ROOM: _____ WIFI: _____ PASSWORD: _____ TV/Remote: _____

TRASH: _____ CLEANING SUPPLIES: _____ VACUUM/MOP: _____

WATER: _____ COFFEE MAKER: _____ FURNACE, A/C: _____

LAUNDRY: _____ DISHWASHER: _____

UTILITY SHUTOFFS: _____ MAIL: _____

PLANT CARE: _____

OTHER: _____

AFTER NOTES: _____

☆ ☆ ☆ ☆ ☆

MEET-UP: _____

Client

NAME: _____ KEY/CODE: _____

ADDRESS: _____ PHONE: _____

STAY DATES/TIMES: _____

STAY DATES/TIMES: _____

STAY DATES/TIMES: _____

NOTES: _____

🐾 Pet Care

PET: _____ DESC: _____

PET: _____ DESC: _____

PET: _____ DESC: _____

PET: _____ DESC: _____

PET: _____ DESC: _____

FEEDING

PET(S): _____ TIME(S): _____ AMOUNT: _____ FOOD: _____

PET(S): _____ TIME(S): _____ AMOUNT: _____ FOOD: _____

PET(S): _____ TIME(S): _____ AMOUNT: _____ FOOD: _____

MEDICATION

PET: _____ MED: _____ DOSE: _____

PET: _____ MED: _____ DOSE: _____

PET: _____ MED: _____ DOSE: _____

PET: _____ MED: _____ DOSE: _____

WALKS: _____ 💩 DISPOSAL: _____

VETERINARIAN: _____

ADDRESS: _____ PHONE: _____

ISSUES: _____

CARE NOTES: _____

HOME CARE 🏠

Where, When &/or How To

EMERGENCY CONTACT: _____

ROOM: _____ WIFI: _____ PASSWORD: _____ TV/Remote: _____

TRASH: _____ CLEANING SUPPLIES: _____ VACUUM/MOP: _____

WATER: _____ COFFEE MAKER: _____ FURNACE, A/C: _____

LAUNDRY: _____ DISHWASHER: _____

UTILITY SHUTOFFS: _____ MAIL: _____

PLANT CARE: _____

OTHER: _____

AFTER NOTES: _____

☆ ☆ ☆ ☆ ☆

Client

NAME: _____
KEY/CODE: _____

ADDRESS: _____
PHONE: _____

STAY DATES/TIMES: _____

STAY DATES/TIMES: _____

STAY DATES/TIMES: _____

NOTES: _____

🐾 Pet Care

PET: _____ DESC: _____

PET: _____ DESC: _____

PET: _____ DESC: _____

PET: _____ DESC: _____

PET: _____ DESC: _____

FEEDING

PET(S): _____ TIME(S): _____ AMOUNT: _____ FOOD: _____

PET(S): _____ TIME(S): _____ AMOUNT: _____ FOOD: _____

PET(S): _____ TIME(S): _____ AMOUNT: _____ FOOD: _____

MEDICATION

PET: _____ MED: _____ DOSE: _____

PET: _____ MED: _____ DOSE: _____

PET: _____ MED: _____ DOSE: _____

PET: _____ MED: _____ DOSE: _____

WALKS: _____ 💩 DISPOSAL: _____

VETERINARIAN: _____

ADDRESS: _____ PHONE: _____

ISSUES: _____

CARE NOTES: _____

HOME CARE 🏠

EMERGENCY CONTACT: _____

Where, When &/or How To

ROOM: _____ WIFI: _____ PASSWORD: _____ TV/Remote: _____

TRASH: _____ CLEANING SUPPLIES: _____ VACUUM/MOP: _____

WATER: _____ COFFEE MAKER: _____ FURNACE, A/C: _____

LAUNDRY: _____ DISHWASHER: _____

UTILITY SHUTOFFS: _____ MAIL: _____

PLANT CARE: _____

OTHER: _____

AFTER NOTES: _____

☆ ☆ ☆ ☆ ☆

MEET-UP: _____

Client

NAME: _____ KEY/CODE: _____

ADDRESS: _____ PHONE: _____

STAY DATES/TIMES: _____

STAY DATES/TIMES: _____

STAY DATES/TIMES: _____

NOTES: _____

🐾 Pet Care

PET: _____ DESC: _____

PET: _____ DESC: _____

PET: _____ DESC: _____

PET: _____ DESC: _____

PET: _____ DESC: _____

FEEDING

PET(S): _____ TIME(S): _____ AMOUNT: _____ FOOD: _____

PET(S): _____ TIME(S): _____ AMOUNT: _____ FOOD: _____

PET(S): _____ TIME(S): _____ AMOUNT: _____ FOOD: _____

MEDICATION

PET: _____ MED: _____ DOSE: _____

PET: _____ MED: _____ DOSE: _____

PET: _____ MED: _____ DOSE: _____

PET: _____ MED: _____ DOSE: _____

WALKS: _____ 💩 DISPOSAL: _____

VETERINARIAN: _____

ADDRESS: _____ PHONE: _____

ISSUES: _____

CARE NOTES: _____

HOME CARE 🏠

Where, When &/or HowTo

EMERGENCY CONTACT: _____

ROOM: _____ WIFI: _____ PASSWORD: _____ TV/Remote: _____

TRASH: _____ CLEANING SUPPLIES: _____ VACUUM/MOP: _____

WATER: _____ COFFEE MAKER: _____ FURNACE, A/C: _____

LAUNDRY: _____ DISHWASHER: _____

UTILITY SHUTOFFS: _____ MAIL: _____

PLANT CARE: _____

OTHER: _____

AFTER NOTES: _____

☆ ☆ ☆ ☆ ☆

Client

MEET-UP: _____

NAME: _____ KEY/CODE: _____

ADDRESS: _____ PHONE: _____

STAY DATES/TIMES: _____

STAY DATES/TIMES: _____

STAY DATES/TIMES: _____

NOTES: _____

🐾 Pet Care

PET: _____ DESC: _____

PET: _____ DESC: _____

PET: _____ DESC: _____

PET: _____ DESC: _____

PET: _____ DESC: _____

FEEDING

PET(S): _____ TIME(S): _____ AMOUNT: _____ FOOD: _____

PET(S): _____ TIME(S): _____ AMOUNT: _____ FOOD: _____

PET(S): _____ TIME(S): _____ AMOUNT: _____ FOOD: _____

MEDICATION

PET: _____ MED: _____ DOSE: _____

PET: _____ MED: _____ DOSE: _____

PET: _____ MED: _____ DOSE: _____

PET: _____ MED: _____ DOSE: _____

WALKS: _____ 💩 DISPOSAL: _____

VETERINARIAN: _____

ADDRESS: _____ PHONE: _____

ISSUES: _____

CARE NOTES: _____

HOME CARE 🏠

Where, When &/or How To

EMERGENCY CONTACT: _____

ROOM: _____ WIFI: _____ PASSWORD: _____ TV/Remote: _____

TRASH: _____ CLEANING SUPPLIES: _____ VACUUM/MOP: _____

WATER: _____ COFFEE MAKER: _____ FURNACE, A/C: _____

LAUNDRY: _____ DISHWASHER: _____

UTILITY SHUTOFFS: _____ MAIL: _____

PLANT CARE: _____

OTHER: _____

AFTER NOTES: _____

☆ ☆ ☆ ☆ ☆

MEET-UP: _____

Client

NAME: _____   KEY/CODE: _____

ADDRESS: _____   PHONE: _____

STAY DATES/TIMES: _____

STAY DATES/TIMES: _____

STAY DATES/TIMES: _____

NOTES: _____

☙ Pet Care

PET:	DESC:	
PET:	DESC:	
PET:	DESC:	
PET:	DESC:	
PET:	DESC:	

FEEDING

PET(S):	TIME(S):	AMOUNT:	FOOD:
PET(S):	TIME(S):	AMOUNT:	FOOD:
PET(S):	TIME(S):	AMOUNT:	FOOD:

MEDICATION

PET:	MED:	DOSE:
PET:	MED:	DOSE:
PET:	MED:	DOSE:
PET:	MED:	DOSE:

WALKS: _____ 💩 DISPOSAL: _____

VETERINARIAN: _____

ADDRESS: _____ PHONE: _____

ISSUES: _____

CARE NOTES: _____

HOME CARE ⌂

Where, When &/or How To

EMERGENCY CONTACT: _____

ROOM:	WIFI:	PASSWORD:	TV/Remote:
TRASH:	CLEANING SUPPLIES:		VACUUM/MOP:
WATER:	COFFEE MAKER:		FURNACE, A/C:
LAUNDRY:			DISHWASHER:
UTILITY SHUTOFFS:			MAIL:

PLANT CARE: _____

OTHER: _____

AFTER NOTES: _____

☆ ☆ ☆ ☆ ☆

Client

MEET-UP: _____

NAME: _____ KEY/CODE: _____

ADDRESS: _____ PHONE: _____

STAY DATES/TIMES: _____

STAY DATES/TIMES: _____

STAY DATES/TIMES: _____

NOTES: _____

🐾 Pet Care

FEEDING

MEDICATION

PET: _____ DESC: _____

PET: _____ DESC: _____

PET: _____ DESC: _____

PET: _____ DESC: _____

PET: _____ DESC: _____

PET(S): _____ TIME(S): _____ AMOUNT: _____ FOOD: _____

PET(S): _____ TIME(S): _____ AMOUNT: _____ FOOD: _____

PET(S): _____ TIME(S): _____ AMOUNT: _____ FOOD: _____

PET: _____ MED: _____ DOSE: _____

PET: _____ MED: _____ DOSE: _____

PET: _____ MED: _____ DOSE: _____

PET: _____ MED: _____ DOSE: _____

WALKS: _____ 💩 DISPOSAL: _____

VETERINARIAN: _____

ADDRESS: _____ PHONE: _____

ISSUES: _____

CARE NOTES: _____

HOME CARE 🏠

Where, When &/or How To

EMERGENCY CONTACT: _____

ROOM: _____ WIFI: _____ PASSWORD: _____ TV/Remote: _____

TRASH: _____ CLEANING SUPPLIES: _____ VACUUM/MOP: _____

WATER: _____ COFFEE MAKER: _____ FURNACE, A/C: _____

LAUNDRY: _____ DISHWASHER: _____

UTILITY SHUTOFFS: _____ MAIL: _____

PLANT CARE: _____

OTHER: _____

AFTER NOTES: _____

☆ ☆ ☆ ☆ ☆

2025

January

S	M	T	W	T	F	S
			1	2	3	4
5	6	7	8	9	10	11
12	13	14	15	16	17	18
19	20	21	22	23	24	25
26	27	28	29	30	31	

February

S	M	T	W	T	F	S
						1
2	3	4	5	6	7	8
9	10	11	12	13	14	15
16	17	18	19	20	21	22
23	24	25	26	27	28	

March

S	M	T	W	T	F	S
						1
2	3	4	5	6	7	8
9	10	11	12	13	14	15
16	17	18	19	20	21	22
23	24	25	26	27	28	29
30	31					

April

S	M	T	W	T	F	S
		1	2	3	4	5
6	7	8	9	10	11	12
13	14	15	16	17	18	19
20	21	22	23	24	25	26
27	28	29	30			

May

S	M	T	W	T	F	S
				1	2	3
4	5	6	7	8	9	10
11	12	13	14	15	16	17
18	19	20	21	22	23	24
25	26	27	28	29	30	31

June

S	M	T	W	T	F	S
1	2	3	4	5	6	7
8	9	10	11	12	13	14
15	16	17	18	19	20	21
22	23	24	25	26	27	28
29	30					

July

S	M	T	W	T	F	S
		1	2	3	4	5
6	7	8	9	10	11	12
13	14	15	16	17	18	19
20	21	22	23	24	25	26
27	28	29	30	31		

August

S	M	T	W	T	F	S
					1	2
3	4	5	6	7	8	9
10	11	12	13	14	15	16
17	18	19	20	21	22	23
24	25	26	27	28	29	30
31						

September

S	M	T	W	T	F	S
	1	2	3	4	5	6
7	8	9	10	11	12	13
14	15	16	17	18	19	20
21	22	23	24	25	26	27
28	29	30				

October

S	M	T	W	T	F	S
			1	2	3	4
5	6	7	8	9	10	11
12	13	14	15	16	17	18
19	20	21	22	23	24	25
26	27	28	29	30	31	

November

S	M	T	W	T	F	S
						1
2	3	4	5	6	7	8
9	10	11	12	13	14	15
16	17	18	19	20	21	22
23	24	25	26	27	28	29
30						

December

S	M	T	W	T	F	S
	1	2	3	4	5	6
7	8	9	10	11	12	13
14	15	16	17	18	19	20
21	22	23	24	25	26	27
28	29	30	31			

2026

January

S	M	T	W	T	F	S
				1	2	3
4	5	6	7	8	9	10
11	12	13	14	15	16	17
18	19	20	21	22	23	24
25	26	27	28	29	30	31

February

S	M	T	W	T	F	S
1	2	3	4	5	6	7
8	9	10	11	12	13	14
15	16	17	18	19	20	21
22	23	24	25	26	27	28

March

S	M	T	W	T	F	S
1	2	3	4	5	6	7
8	9	10	11	12	13	14
15	16	17	18	19	20	21
22	23	24	25	26	27	28
29	30	31				

April

S	M	T	W	T	F	S
			1	2	3	4
5	6	7	8	9	10	11
12	13	14	15	16	17	18
19	20	21	22	23	24	25
26	27	28	29	30		

May

S	M	T	W	T	F	S
					1	2
3	4	5	6	7	8	9
10	11	12	13	14	15	16
17	18	19	20	21	22	23
24	25	26	27	28	29	30
31						

June

S	M	T	W	T	F	S
	1	2	3	4	5	6
7	8	9	10	11	12	13
14	15	16	17	18	19	20
21	22	23	24	25	26	27
28	29	30				

July

S	M	T	W	T	F	S
			1	2	3	4
5	6	7	8	9	10	11
12	13	14	15	16	17	18
19	20	21	22	23	24	25
26	27	28	29	30	31	

August

S	M	T	W	T	F	S
						1
2	3	4	5	6	7	8
9	10	11	12	13	14	15
16	17	18	19	20	21	22
23	24	25	26	27	28	29
30	31					

September

S	M	T	W	T	F	S
		1	2	3	4	5
6	7	8	9	10	11	12
13	14	15	16	17	18	19
20	21	22	23	24	25	26
27	28	29	30			

October

S	M	T	W	T	F	S
				1	2	3
4	5	6	7	8	9	10
11	12	13	14	15	16	17
18	19	20	21	22	23	24
25	26	27	28	29	30	31

November

S	M	T	W	T	F	S
1	2	3	4	5	6	7
8	9	10	11	12	13	14
15	16	17	18	19	20	21
22	23	24	25	26	27	28
29	30					

December

S	M	T	W	T	F	S
		1	2	3	4	5
6	7	8	9	10	11	12
13	14	15	16	17	18	19
20	21	22	23	24	25	26
27	28	29	30	31		

December 2024

Sunday	Monday	Tuesday	Wednesday	Thursday	Friday	Saturday
1	2	3	4	5	6	7
8	9	10	11	12	13	14
15	16	17	18	19	20	21
22	23	24	25	26	27	28
29	30	31	1	2	3	4

NOTES:
_____
_____
_____
_____

January 2025

Sunday	Monday	Tuesday	Wednesday	Thursday	Friday	Saturday
29	30	31	1	2	3	4
5	6	7	8	9	10	11
12	13	14	15	16	17	18
19	20	21	22	23	24	25
26	27	28	29	30	31	1

NOTES:

February 2025

Sunday	Monday	Tuesday	Wednesday	Thursday	Friday	Saturday
26	27	28	29	30	31	1
2	3	4	5	6	7	8
9	10	11	12	13	14	15
16	17	18	19	20	21	22
23	24	25	26	27	28	1

NOTES: _____

_____

_____

_____

March 2025

Sunday	Monday	Tuesday	Wednesday	Thursday	Friday	Saturday
23	24	25	26	27	28	1
2	3	4	5	6	7	8
9	10	11	12	13	14	15
16	17	18	19	20	21	22
23	24	25	26	27	28	29
30	31	1	2	3	4	5

NOTES:

April 2025

Sunday	Monday	Tuesday	Wednesday	Thursday	Friday	Saturday
30	31	1	2	3	4	5
6	7	8	9	10	11	12
13	14	15	16	17	18	19
20	21	22	23	24	25	26
27	28	29	30	1	2	3

NOTES: _____

_____

_____

_____

May 2025

Sunday	Monday	Tuesday	Wednesday	Thursday	Friday	Saturday
27	28	29	30	1	2	3
4	5	6	7	8	9	10
11	12	13	14	15	16	17
18	19	20	21	22	23	24
25	26	27	28	29	30	31

NOTES:

June 2025

Sunday	Monday	Tuesday	Wednesday	Thursday	Friday	Saturday
1	2	3	4	5	6	7
8	9	10	11	12	13	14
15	16	17	18	19	20	21
22	23	24	25	26	27	28
29	30	1	2	3	4	5

NOTES: _____

_____

_____

_____

July 2025

Sunday	Monday	Tuesday	Wednesday	Thursday	Friday	Saturday
29	30	1	2	3	4	5
6	7	8	9	10	11	12
13	14	15	16	17	18	19
20	21	22	23	24	25	26
27	28	29	30	31	1	2

NOTES:

August 2025

Sunday	Monday	Tuesday	Wednesday	Thursday	Friday	Saturday
27	28	29	30	31	1	2
3	4	5	6	7	8	9
10	11	12	13	14	15	16
17	18	19	20	21	22	23
24	25	26	27	28	29	30
31	1	2	3	4	5	6

NOTES:
_____
_____
_____
_____

September 2025

Sunday	Monday	Tuesday	Wednesday	Thursday	Friday	Saturday
31	1	2	3	4	5	6
7	8	9	10	11	12	13
14	15	16	17	18	19	20
21	22	23	24	25	26	27
28	29	30	1	2	3	4

NOTES:
_____
_____
_____
_____

October 2025

Sunday	Monday	Tuesday	Wednesday	Thursday	Friday	Saturday
28	29	30	1	2	3	4
5	6	7	8	9	10	11
12	13	14	15	16	17	18
19	20	21	22	23	24	25
26	27	28	29	30	31	1

NOTES:

November 2025

Sunday	Monday	Tuesday	Wednesday	Thursday	Friday	Saturday
26	27	28	29	30	31	1
2	3	4	5	6	7	8
9	10	11	12	13	14	15
16	17	18	19	20	21	22
23	24	25	26	27	28	29
30	1	2	3	4	5	6

NOTES:

December 2025

Sunday	Monday	Tuesday	Wednesday	Thursday	Friday	Saturday
30	1	2	3	4	5	6
7	8	9	10	11	12	13
14	15	16	17	18	19	20
21	22	23	24	25	26	27
28	29	30	31	1	2	3

NOTES: _____

_____

_____

_____

January 2026

Sunday	Monday	Tuesday	Wednesday	Thursday	Friday	Saturday
28	29	30	31	1	2	3
4	5	6	7	8	9	10
11	12	13	14	15	16	17
18	19	20	21	22	23	24
25	26	27	28	29	30	31

NOTES:

February 2026

Sunday	Monday	Tuesday	Wednesday	Thursday	Friday	Saturday
1	2	3	4	5	6	7
8	9	10	11	12	13	14
15	16	17	18	19	20	21
22	23	24	25	26	27	28

NOTES:

March 2026

Sunday	Monday	Tuesday	Wednesday	Thursday	Friday	Saturday
1	2	3	4	5	6	7
8	9	10	11	12	13	14
15	16	17	18	19	20	21
22	23	24	25	26	27	28
29	30	31	1	2	3	4

NOTES: _____

_____

_____

_____

April 2026

Sunday	Monday	Tuesday	Wednesday	Thursday	Friday	Saturday
29	30	31	1	2	3	4
5	6	7	8	9	10	11
12	13	14	15	16	17	18
19	20	21	22	23	24	25
26	27	28	29	30	1	2

NOTES: _____

_____

_____

_____

May 2026

Sunday	Monday	Tuesday	Wednesday	Thursday	Friday	Saturday
26	27	28	29	30	1	2
3	4	5	6	7	8	9
10	11	12	13	14	15	16
17	18	19	20	21	22	23
24	25	26	27	28	29	30
31	1	2	3	4	5	6

NOTES:

June 2026

Sunday	Monday	Tuesday	Wednesday	Thursday	Friday	Saturday
31	1	2	3	4	5	6
7	8	9	10	11	12	13
14	15	16	17	18	19	20
21	22	23	24	25	26	27
28	29	30	1	2	3	4

NOTES: _____

_____

_____

_____

July 2026

Sunday	Monday	Tuesday	Wednesday	Thursday	Friday	Saturday
28	29	30	1	2	3	4
5	6	7	8	9	10	11
12	13	14	15	16	17	18
19	20	21	22	23	24	25
26	27	28	29	30	31	1

NOTES:

August 2026

Sunday	Monday	Tuesday	Wednesday	Thursday	Friday	Saturday
26	27	28	29	30	31	1
2	3	4	5	6	7	8
9	10	11	12	13	14	15
16	17	18	19	20	21	22
23	24	25	26	27	28	29
30	31	1	2	3	4	5

NOTES: _____

_____

_____

_____

September 2026

Sunday	Monday	Tuesday	Wednesday	Thursday	Friday	Saturday
30	31	1	2	3	4	5
6	7	8	9	10	11	12
13	14	15	16	17	18	19
20	21	22	23	24	25	26
27	28	29	30	1	2	3

NOTES: _____

_____

_____

_____

October 2026

Sunday	Monday	Tuesday	Wednesday	Thursday	Friday	Saturday
27	28	29	30	1	2	3
4	5	6	7	8	9	10
11	12	13	14	15	16	17
18	19	20	21	22	23	24
25	26	27	28	29	30	31

NOTES:

November 2026

Sunday	Monday	Tuesday	Wednesday	Thursday	Friday	Saturday
1	2	3	4	5	6	7
8	9	10	11	12	13	14
15	16	17	18	19	20	21
22	23	24	25	26	27	28
29	30	1	2	3	4	5

NOTES: _____
_____
_____
_____

December 2026

Sunday	Monday	Tuesday	Wednesday	Thursday	Friday	Saturday
29	30	1	2	3	4	5
6	7	8	9	10	11	12
13	14	15	16	17	18	19
20	21	22	23	24	25	26
27	28	29	30	31	1	2

NOTES:

January 2027

Sunday	Monday	Tuesday	Wednesday	Thursday	Friday	Saturday
27	28	29	30	31	1	2
3	4	5	6	7	8	9
10	11	12	13	14	15	16
17	18	19	20	21	22	23
24	25	26	27	28	29	30
31	1	2	3	4	5	6

NOTES:

CONTACTS

Name

Address

City   State   Zip

Phone

Email

Name

Address

City   State   Zip

Phone

Email

Name

Address

City   State   Zip

Phone

Email

Name

Address

City   State   Zip

Phone

Email

Name

Address

City   State   Zip

Phone

Email

Name

Address

City   State   Zip

Phone

Email

Name

Address

City   State   Zip

Phone

Email

Name

Address

City   State   Zip

Phone

Email

CONTACTS

Name

Address

City   State   Zip

Phone

Email

Name

Address

City   State   Zip

Phone

Email

Name

Address

City   State   Zip

Phone

Email

Name

Address

City   State   Zip

Phone

Email

Name

Address

City   State   Zip

Phone

Email

Name

Address

City   State   Zip

Phone

Email

Name

Address

City   State   Zip

Phone

Email

Name

Address

City   State   Zip

Phone

Email

CONTACTS

Name

Address

City   State   Zip

Phone

Email

Name

Address

City   State   Zip

Phone

Email

Name

Address

City   State   Zip

Phone

Email

Name

Address

City   State   Zip

Phone

Email

Name

Address

City   State   Zip

Phone

Email

Name

Address

City   State   Zip

Phone

Email

Name

Address

City   State   Zip

Phone

Email

Name

Address

City   State   Zip

Phone

Email

CONTACTS

Name

Address

City   State   Zip

Phone

Email

Name

Address

City   State   Zip

Phone

Email

Name

Address

City   State   Zip

Phone

Email

Name

Address

City   State   Zip

Phone

Email

Name

Address

City   State   Zip

Phone

Email

Name

Address

City   State   Zip

Phone

Email

Name

Address

City   State   Zip

Phone

Email

Name

Address

City   State   Zip

Phone

Email

NOTES:
_____

NOTES:

NOTES:

NOTES:

NOTES:

NOTES:

NOTES:

NOTES:

NOTES:

NOTES:

Discover more great books from
Nola Lee Kelsey & Soggy Nomad Press

Zoology: Word
Searches & Games for
the Naturalist's Soul
979-8-9855011-1-7

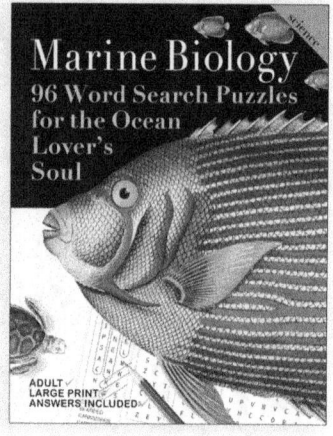

Marine Biology: 96
Word Search Puzzles for
the Ocean Lover's Soul
979-8-9855011-4-8

Ornithology: 112 Word
Search Puzzles for the
Bird Lover's Soul
979-8-9855011-2-4

Primatology: Word
Search Puzzles for the
Naturalist's Soul
978-1-957532-36-3

Herpetology: Word
Search Puzzles for the
Naturalist's Soul
979-8-9855011-5-5

Mammalogy: 101 Word
Search Puzzle's for the
Naturalist's Soul
979-8-9855011-3-1

Invertebrates: 92 Word
Search Puzzles for the
Naturalists Soul
978-1-957532-99-8

World Travel Word
Searches
979-8-985501-16-2

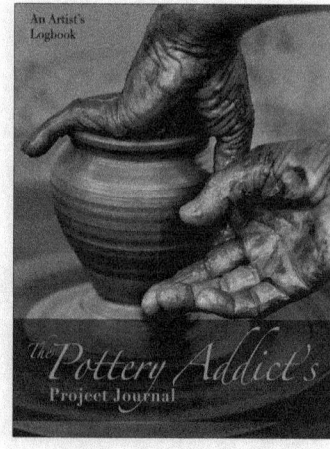

The Pottery Addict's
Project Journal: An
Artist's Logbook
978-1-957532-00-4

The Ultimate
Boondocker's
Dispersed Camping
Logbook &Journal
978-1-957532-35-6

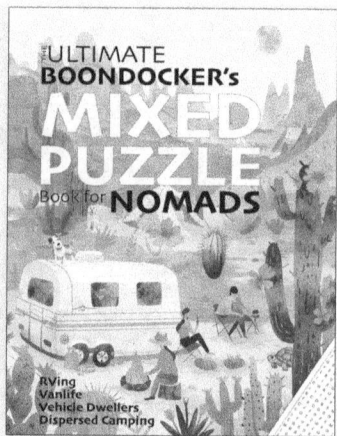

The Ultimate
Boondocker's Mixed
Puzzle Book for Nomads
978-1-957532-42-4

USA Travel Word
Searches
979-8-9855011-0-0

Discover more books from
Nola Lee Kelsey & Soggy Nomad Press

The Crazy Dog Lady's
Activity Book for Adults
978-1-957532-37-0

The Crazy Cat Lady's
Activity Book for Adults
978-1-957532-07-3

The Crazy Cat Lady's
Activity Book #2
978-1-957532-53-0

The Crazy Cat Lady's
Coloring Book
for Adults
978-1-957532-27-7

The Crazy Chicken
Lady's Activity
Book for Adults
78-1-957532-27-1

Mythical & Magical
Creatures Activity
Book for Adults
978-1-957532-33-2

The Fabulous Las
Vegas Activity Book
for Adults
978-1-957532-40-0

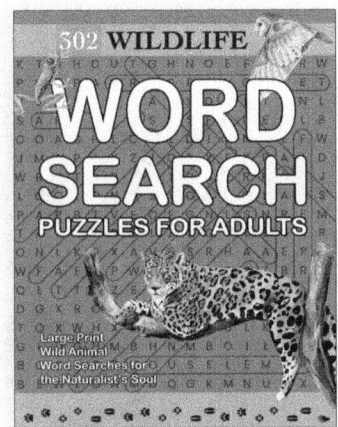

302 Wildlife Word
Search Puzzles for
Adults
978-1-957532-04-2

Easy & Relaxing Word
Search Puzzles for
Adults
978-1-957532-41-7

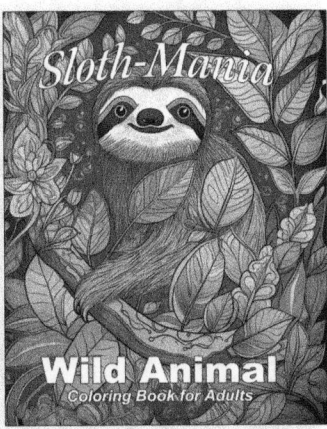

Sloth-Mania Wild
Animal Coloring Book
for Adults
978-1-957532-31-8

My First Sentences:
Writing Practice and
Activity Pages
978-1-957532-05-9

Snarky Cats Stealing
Quotes Coloring Book
for Adults
978-1-957532-18-9

Support Small Press Publications

Please recommend *The Pet Sitting Professional's Organizer & Log Book* **to other caregivers, suggest it in forums and leave honest reviews.**

*New editions with updated calendars will be released each October.

www.ingramcontent.com/pod-product-compliance
Lightning Source LLC
Chambersburg PA
CBHW081336120626
46546CB00011B/3376